Powerful prayers for different situations

VOLUME ONE

SYLVIA SAMMS

© Copyright Sylvia Samms 2022

This book is sold subject to the conditions: it is not, by way of trade or otherwise, lent, hired out or otherwise circulated in any form of binding or cover other than that in which it is published. No part of this publication may be reproduced, stored in a retrieval system or transmitted in any form or by any means (electronic, mechanical, photocopying, recording or otherwise) without prior written permission from the Publisher.

FIRST EDITION

ISBN: 978-1-7397428-4-3 (Paperback)

It Is Time To Pray

Sylvia Samms

For more information, please direct your emails to:

info@ibelieveican.co.uk

IT IS TIME TO PRAY.

This prayer book is dedicated to all people – all races, creeds and nationalities.

We can agree that we are now living in challenging times, and we all need help from the Lord at all times.

As we read, let us pray and raise our expectations to be empowered by the Holy Spirit of God. Let us be encouraged to put our trust in God, to meet our needs in agreement with: **Philippians 4:19** *But my God shall supply all your needs according to his riches in glory by Christ Jesus.*

Beloved ones, let us read this powerful prayer book expecting to receive some super natural blessings from the Lord such as : healing, strength, comfort, peace, courage, confidence, inspiration, wisdom, knowledge, understanding, revelation, discernment, discretion and so much more.

Let us declare **Psalm 119:105** over our lives: Lord, *"Thy word is a lamp unto my feet and a light unto my path."*

Lord, I am determined to walk in the light of your word so that I will not stumble and fall. I refuse to walk in darkness because it is the plan of the wicked one, the devil.

Today I declare, that where there is weakness, I declare strength. Where there are discouragements, I declare encouragement. Lord, where there is sickness, I declare healing in the mighty exalted name of Jesus Christ.

I will always speak positive words over our lives and build up my confidence and my relationship with the God that created me. I will always have a glorious relationship with Him because he is my King, and my redeemer. Lord, today I declare that I am dedicating my life to you.

Contents

Introduction	1
Tips For Prayer	4

MORNING PRAYERS

Sunday Morning Prayer	7
Monday Morning Prayer	9
Tuesday Morning Prayer	11
Wednesday Morning Prayer	13
Thursday Morning Prayer	15
Friday Morning Prayer	17
Saturday Morning Prayer	19
General Morning Prayer - Part 1	21
General Morning Prayer - Part 2	23

WHY WE PRAY

Why We Pray - Part 1	26
Why We Pray - Part 2	29

PRAYER FOR PEACE

Pray for the peace of Jerusalem	32
Prayer of Thanksgiving for God's grace	34
Thanksgiving for My Personal Connection to God	36

PRAYER FOR GOOD HEALTH

Prayer for my Healing - Part 1	38
Prayer for my Healing - Part 2	40

Personal Prayer - Part 1   42
Personal Prayer - Part 2   44

PRAYER FOR LEADERS

Prayer for Spiritual Leaders - Part 1   46
Prayer for Spiritual Leaders - Part 2   48
Prayer for the Government - Part 1   50
Prayer for the Government - Part 2   52

PRAYER FOR YOUNG PEOPLE

Prayer for Young Godly Men Who Are Seeking a Wife   54
Prayer for Young Women in General   56
Prayer for Young Men in General - Part 1   58
Prayer for Young Men in General - Part 2   60
Prayer for Godly Young Women Who Desire to Be Married   62
Prayer for My Community   64

PRAYER FOR OUR COMMUNITY

Prayer for My Healing   66
Prayer for the Bereaved   68

PRAYER FOR THE CHILDREN

A Parent's Prayer for Their Unborn Baby   71
Prayer for the Children - Part 1   73
Prayer for the Children - Part 2   75

PRAYER FOR PEACE

Prayer for Peace - Part 1   78
Prayer for Peace - Part 2   80
Prayer for Peace - Part 3   82
Prayer for Protection   84

Prayer of Assurance in God 86
Prayer for a Change of Heart 88

PRAYER FOR GOOD HEALTH

Prayer of Thanksgiving for a New Heart 90
Prayer for Good Health - Part 1 93
Prayer for Good Health - Part 2 95
Prayer for Healthcare 97

PRAYER FOR VICTORY OVER DEPRESSION

Prayer for Victory Over Depression 100

PRAYER FOR THE CHURCH

Prayer for the Church - Part 1 103
Prayer for the Church - Part 2 105
Prayer for the Church - Part 3 107
Prayer for Discernment 109
Prayer for the Police Force 112
Prayer for Those Who Are in Prison 114

PRAYER FOR THOSE WHO ARE TAKING EXAMS

Prayer for Those Who Are Taking Exams 117

PRAYER FOR THE HOMELESS

Prayer for the Homeless 120

PRAYER FOR MARRIAGES

Prayer for Marriages 123
Prayer for Husband & Wife - Part 1 125

Prayer for Husband & Wife - Part 2	127
Prayer for Husband & Wife - Part 3	129
Prayer for Husband & Wife - Part 4	131
Thanksgiving for Husband & Wife Praying Together	133
Prayer for My Home & Family	135

PRAYER AGAINST SPIRITUAL WARFARE

Prayer Against Spiritual Warfare - Part 1	137
Prayer Against Spiritual Warfare - Part 2	139
Prayer Against Demonic Attack - Part 1	141
Prayer Against Demonic Attack - Part 2	143
Prayer for God's Help	145

PRAYER FOR A FRIEND

Prayer for a Friend Who is Sick	147
Today I am Receiving My Miracle	149

THERE IS A HIGHER POWER

There is a Higher Power Than Our Natural Power	151
Praise & Worship to the God of Heaven	153
The Love of God in Action	155
Words of Hope - Part 1	157
Words of Hope - Part 2	159
Protection in Jesus Christ	161
Thanksgiving for God's Promises	163
Some Meanings to Life	165
Only God Knows the Real Me	167
Believing in the True & Living God - Part 1	169
Believing in the True & Living God - Part 2	171
By the Grace of God I Speak to my Body	173
Saying a Prayer Before we Eat Our Meals	175

DECLARATIONS BY FAITH

Declarations by Faith - Part 1	178
Declarations by Faith - Part 2	180
Declarations by Faith - Part 3	182
Declarations by Faith - Part 4	184
Declarations by Faith - Part 5	186
A Selection of Bible Verses of God's Promises	188
A Selection of Bible Verses Referring to Jesus	190

REMEMBER THAT GOD IS IN CONTROL

Remember that God is in Control	193
Blessings	195
Conclusion - It is Time to Pray, Prayer Book	197
Acknowledgements	198
About The Author	199
Analysing	202
Bibliography	205
Bible Citations	206
Notes	219

Introduction

IT is a good time to pray and to give thanks unto the Lord, for He is good, His mercy endures forever.

IT IS TIME TO PRAY. This prayer book is designed to help everyone, as we can all receive many benefits when we pray.

Prayer is a powerful tool that we can use, to strengthen the weak, to heal broken lives, and to give restoration and comfort to the sad and the lonely and so much more.

When we pray, God gives us a better understanding of life; prayer gives us confidence of who God is to us. Prayer helps us to know how we can receive benefits from the Lord. Prayer of faith can heal Physical, emotional and mental pain. Prayer gives sight to the spiritually blind, hope to the hopeless, strength to the weak, courage to the discouraged, restoration, and so much more.

Prayer is like a seed with healing properties, it can heal broken hearts and broken lives. Prayer is like a water tank; it can water the souls of man to produce physical and spiritual growth.

Whether you are a believer or a nonbeliever, this is the prayer book for you to read. Read this prayer book believing in God, trusting in God and depending on God. This is a privilege for you to increase your faith in God and watch what God will do for you. Read this prayer book and increase your faith in God to empower you with a desire to change your life. Read this prayer book and you will also have a new relationship with the true and living God, our creator.

2 Peter 3:9 teaches us that: *The Lord is not slack (slow) concerning his promise, as some men count slackness; but is long-suffering to us-ward, not willing that any should perish, but that all should come to repentance.* This means that God will keep his promises to us; he wants us to have a life with a new relationship with him.

Prayer is one of the most important ways that we can talk to Jesus Christ. Even though we cannot see him with our natural eyes, let us pray believing and trusting in God. He will help us to make that change from an old lifestyle to a new lifestyle. Anyone can pray to God. I am encouraging you to read-

Ephesians 4:22-32*. These words have helped me to understand the purpose for my life, what I should or should not embrace.

The Holy Scriptures is the word of God, and it is His road map for all of us to read, so we can receive deeper revelations from him.

There is life in the word of God.

All scripture verses with the symbol * are written in the "Bible Citations " at the back of the book.

*Full scripture: Ephesians 4: 22-32 [Bible Citations: pg 206]

Tips For Prayer

PRAY believing, trusting and depending on God.
PRAY in faith, and without doubting.
PRAY in thanksgiving and honour to God.
PRAY in commitment and perseverance.
PRAY in the spirit with the love of God in your heart.
PRAY in obedience, honesty, humility and willingness.
PRAY in the Holy Spirit.
PRAY in fasting and supplication.
PRAY in the name of the Lord Jesus Christ.
PRAY and raise your expectations to receive from God.
PRAY and refresh yourself in the Almighty God.
PRAY and acknowledge God as the only true source to meet all of your needs.
PRAY and wait upon God to answer your prayer according to His divine will.
PRAY and build your relationship with God, and you will get good results.
PRAY reminding God of His promises.
PRAY with a determination to build your relationship with God.
PRAY with respect to God and reverence Him.
PRAY with a true heart of forgivingness.
PRAY using the words of God and come in agreement with the word.
PRAY on a regularly basis.
PRAY for all people.

Jesus said in **John 13:34:** *A new commandment I give unto you. That ye love one another; as I have loved you that ye also love one another.*

Jesus said in **Mark 11:25-26:** *²⁵ And when ye stand praying, forgive, if ye have aught (hold anything) against any; that your Father also which is in heaven may forgive you your trespasses.*

²⁶ But if ye do not forgive, neither will your Father which is in heaven forgive your trespasses.

These are very important commandments. Let us all take notice and obey. Let us love each other and forgive those who hurt us, because we also needs love and forgiveness from the Lord.

Sunday Morning Prayer

PSALM 118:24

This is the day, which the LORD hath made; we will rejoice and be glad in it.

LORD, this is the first day of the week, I will rejoice in this day and I will be glad. I am so thankful that you have preserved my life to see this day. I thank you Lord that you have given me a new assignment today. By your grace, nothing shall defeat me in this day. I am safe; and secured because your divine blood is protecting me. Lord, I believe that your powerful hands are capable to help me to carry out this assignment for your glory, O mighty God.

Lord, I thank you for safety. I thank you for good health. I thank you that you have appointed and anointed me to function by your Holy Spirit. Father, I am committed to perform all the assignments that you have assigned for me to do in the mighty name of Jesus. Almighty God, by your grace help me to be willing, and to be committed to fulfil all that you have called me to do.

Lord, by your grace you have given me power and authority to do your will. You have given me legal rights to speak your words to cast out every force of darkness that may want to attack my family or me. In the mighty name of Jesus Christ, I receive your power to command every force to return to the pit of hell and remain there.

This morning I walk in the Spirit, by the power of the living God. I live by the word of God to accomplish the work that you have assigned me to do in the mighty name of Jesus.

According to *1 Peter 3:12* your words said: *For the eyes of the Lord are over the righteous, and his ears are open unto their prayers: but the face of the Lord is against them that do evil.*

Lord, I put my trust in you that you will help me to do that, which is right. Lord, please empower me to live and perform your word in my life.

Holy God, I pray for the elderly and the children that are suffering, for whatever reason. I ask that you would release and send me or someone else with a good and generous heart, to help the vulnerable. Provide for them financially, physically, emotionally and mentally. Lord, please help them to come to know you as their only source of salvation.

Merciful Father, I believe that your eyes are always upon us and you will always hear and answer prayers.

O Lord God, I praise your Holy name this morning for hearing and answering my prayer of faith. In the name of Jesus Christ, I pray.

Amen.

Monday Morning Prayer

PSALM 34:1

I will bless the LORD at all times: his praise
shall continually be in my mouth.

LORD, as my family and I start this new day, we rise to praise your holy exalted name, for you alone are LORD. Mighty God, we bow our knees before you this morning, and we hail you King of Kings and Lord of Lords. We declare **Psalm 34:1** over our lives. We will worship you at all times and your praise shall always be in our mouth.

Lord, I thank you for calling my family and me to your throne room to pray. We open up our heart's door to you, and we welcome your anointing power in our lives. Lord, we ask you to empower us to worship and adore you at all times.

Lord, as a family, we thank you for your love, mercy and compassion. We ask that your grace and mercy will protect us and keep us safe throughout this day and always.

Eternal God, this morning by faith we position every parent and child in this neighbourhood, and the nations, into your care. Lord, please build a firewall of protection around every one of us wherever we are this morning.

Almighty God, we take this opportunity to pray for the safety and help for the elderly. Lord, we pray for the school children as they journey to and from school each day. We pray for the parents and teachers that they will have patience and endurance to cope with the children. Lord please protect all road users and those who travel to and from work daily. We pray for strength and safety for everyone.

Mighty God, we pray against every attack of the enemies. We pray for peace and good health, and that you will grant every one of us favours in our everyday lives. Lord we pray for financial help to pay for food and to pay the bills.

Lord, help everyone to look to you for your divine help. O Lord God, only in you we are safe, only in you we are secure, only in you we have peace. We pray that everyone will come to know you as Lord and Saviour.

O Lord God, we thank you for hearing and answering our prayer of faith in the name of Jesus we pray.

Amen.

Tuesday Morning Prayer

PSALM 27:1

The LORD is my light and my salvation; whom shall I fear? The Lord is the strength of my life; of whom shall I be afraid?

LORD, I thank you this morning that I can rise from my bed with the confidence and the assurance that you are my light and my salvation, and for this reason I shall not fear.

Lord, you are my Alpha and you are my Omega, the beginning and my ending. You are my first and my last. Lord you are everything to me.

I shall not fear, because you are the only one keeping me and strengthening me daily, you are the one protecting and guiding my family and me and we shall not be afraid. Today I walk in victory and not defeat. I walk by faith and not by sight. I walk in the light and not in darkness, for your words have brought light into my life.

Lord Jesus, this morning I walk expecting favours from you, and from man. Nothing shall be lacking in my life or my family's life. No confusing or tormenting spirit shall invade my family, my home or anything in our possession.

Holy God, I have confidence that when I call upon the name of Jesus Christ, you are protecting me and I shall not be afraid. When I call upon your blood of Jesus Christ, you will subdue, tear down and destroy every plan and every strategy of the enemies on my behalf.

I receive perfect peace this morning. I declare that I am an overcomer by the blood of Jesus. Sovereign Lord, I am convinced that you are Lord all by yourself and you are leading my family and me in the right direction throughout our lives. Hallelujah, praise God Almighty.

Lord, I thank you for hearing and answering my prayers. In the name of Jesus, I pray.

Amen.

Wednesday Morning Prayer

ISAIAH 53:5

But he was wounded for our transgressions, he was bruised for our iniquities: the chastisement of our peace was upon him; and with his stripes we are healed.

This is the day that the Lord hath made, I will rejoice and be glad in this day. It is a day of thanksgiving and praise to the Most High God. It is a day to glorify and to exalt the name of Jesus. Lord, I thank you for this beautiful day. It is a day of new beginnings for my family and me. It is a day of grace and favours. Lord, it is a day of healing and blessing.

I give thanks and praise to you Lord Jesus, that you were willing to suffer such a horrible death, for my healing and my salvation. Today I am receiving the benefit of your peace. Praise God.

O Lord, I am thankful, I am grateful that you stand in my place. I cannot repay you for what you have done for me. Lord, this morning I rise to praise you. I rise to worship you. I give you all the honour and the glory that is due unto to your name.

I receive my peace and my healing this morning, in the mighty name of Jesus Christ. I command every sickness and every form of dysfunction to leave my body. I command every part of my body to function, just as God has designed it to function right now. This morning, I declare that by the stripes of Jesus Christ I am healed from every sickness and every disease.

I command my body to line up with the word of God and live in good health. I command my mind to be stable and think positive. I command my eyes to see God's grace in action in my life.

I believe that God's word is true and I am receiving more of God every day. I believe that God's word is powerful enough to break every form of discomfort, to dismantle every chain or rope of sickness; I speak the word of God to perform every kind of healing in my body right now.

In the mighty name of Jesus Christ, I pray.

Amen.

Thursday Morning Prayer

PHILIPPIANS 4:7

And the Peace of God, which passeth all understanding, shall keep your hearts and minds through Christ Jesus.

MIGHTY God, gracious God, you are sovereign over your creation. This morning I rise to worship you and to magnify your Holy, exalted name. Lord, no one can survive without you. If you didn't wake us out of our sleep this morning, we could not wake ourselves. If you didn't give us oxygen to breathe, no one could survive or live. Lord, I am thankful, and I am grateful, for your daily provisions towards us.

Lord God, as I start this new day, I embrace your divine peace according to ***Philippians 4:7.***

Your word said: *And the peace of God that passeth all understanding shall keep your heart and minds through Christ Jesus.*

I thank you that your peace will keep my heart and my mind even though I may not understand how it works, but I have confidence in you to perform what you say. Merciful God, please help me never to take your word for granted. Your peace is a precious gift of moral life values. Lord, please continue to shine your light of peace in me, around me, and through me.

Father, help me to always be aware that it is you who has favoured me, to give me this heavenly treasure of your peace, to comfort me in times of brokenness and sadness, in times of distress and despair. In times when it seems as if there is no hope, Lord, your peace will embrace me.

Today I purpose in my heart to secure your perfect peace Lord please strengthen me and console me. Lord I am certain that the power of your Holy Spirit is empowering me daily, with your supernatural Peace that is embracing me to trust in you. Father God, in spite of my weakness I thank you for the blessing of your peace.

I declare the Peace of God to continue to cover my family and cover me right now. Cover our mind. Lord, cover our positions, and our home. Merciful God, when sorrow surrounds us, and when it seems as if there is no hope Lord, we refuse to accept the spirit of confusion and torment. I ask that you will cover us with your divine blanket of your divine peace.

Eternal God, help us not to allow our emotions or anyone to rob us of your peace. In the mighty name of Jesus Christ of Nazareth, I pray.

Amen.

Friday Morning Prayer

JOHN 14:27

Peace I leave with you, my peace I give unto you: not as the world giveth, give I unto you. Let not your heart be troubled, neither let it be afraid.

LORD, this morning I declare that you are more precious than silver. Lord, you are more costly than gold. Lord, you are more beautiful than diamonds, and there is no one or nothing that I should desire or compare to you. Almighty God, gracious God, you are sovereign over the universe. I thank you, O Lord, that this morning you have given me a word that is able to sustain and keep me throughout my life.

I receive this word into my spirit this morning. This word of peace is my signpost directing me today. I shall not be distracted or diverted. I shall not allow anyone or anything to confuse my mind today, because your word is leading me and I am willing to follow.

Lord, by the power of your Holy Spirit, I use the power of your word to tear down and destroy every lying and deceiving word of the enemy; I destroy and dismantle every contrary word from the enemy. I refuse to accommodate the deceptions of the world that you did not give to me; they are counterfeits and a distraction to produce defeat. The lying words of the enemy are false evidence that are appearing to be real.

Mighty God of creation, I am holding on to your word. I am treasuring the peace of your word. Lord, this morning I am lavishing myself in your perfect peace and I shall overcome every negative word of the enemies.

God of Abraham, Isaac and Jacob, you have planted me beside the rivers of water, and I am now bearing fruit in its season. My leaves shall not whither and whatsoever I do, I shall always prosper because your peace lives inside of me. I am victorious. Praise God, praise God.

Father, I am so thankful that you have considered me. You have taken away all confusions, and you have given me your perfect peace. Hallelujah, glory to God.

I praise your Holy, exalted name. Lord Jesus, I thank you for hearing and answering my prayers of faith. Hallelujah, praise God.

Amen.

Saturday Morning Prayer

PSALM 133:1-2

¹Behold, how good and how pleasant it is for brethren to dwell together in unity! ²It is like the precious ointment upon the head, that ran down upon the beard, even Aaron's beard: that went down to the skirts of his garments.

LORD GOD of Abraham, Isaac and Jacob, this morning I come to you in the spirit of thanksgiving. You are the great God of grace. You are powerful, mighty and strong, you are the God that supports unity for It is pleasant in your sight. Lord, you know how wonderful and powerful it is when we live in the unity of your word, and how much we can achieve when brethren (people) or families are embracing unity.

This morning I call my immediate family, my church family and everyone in my neighbourhood to the place of prayer. I ask that your anointing oil will pour over and into every one of us. Lord, I am aware that the anointing of your Holy Spirit is capable to break yokes, barriers, and every stronghold of the enemy.

Gracious God, today I declare unity in my home, in my families, in the places of worship, in the community where I live and in my place of work. Father, I ask that you will raise us up with your love, so that we will be labourers together into your vineyard Lord, help us to sow seeds of kindness, mercy and compassion so that when you return you will reap a good harvest.

I declare that the anointing oil of your Holy Spirit to take control and drive out every dis-unity and malfunctioning spirit that is not of you. I declare that the unity of your Holy Spirit will be identified in all believers so we can make a difference in this world. Lord just like the anointing oil that was poured out upon Aaron, the High Priest, so that he could function spiritually to serve in the tabernacle. Lord, please let Your Holy Spirit transform us for your service.

Lord, this morning I ask that your anointing oil will saturate us and prepare us to serve you and others that are in need. Let the spirit of unity be the chain and the rope that draws us closer to you as we serve in the area that you have assigned to us.

Lord, please let our lives be bound together with pleasantness and cheerfulness to do your will, in the mighty name of Jesus Christ of Nazareth I pray.

Amen.

General Morning Prayer - Part 1

1 JOHN 5: 14-15

14 And this is the confidence that we have in him, that, if we ask anything according to his will, he heareth us: 15 And if we know that he hear us, whatsoever we ask, we know that we have the petitions that we desired of him.

O LORD God Almighty, it is with great confidence that I face this new day. I thank you for your goodness, kindness and faithfulness. I give honour to your Holy exalted name, for you are gracious and your mercies endure forever.

Lord, I thank you for giving me the confidence to ask you for your favours for every inhabitant of the earth. Father, help us all to acknowledge you and put our trust in you. Help us to honour and respect you, for you are our life giver. Mighty God, increase our faith, help us to understand that you are in control of our lives and you are the one who provides for us.

According to **Psalm 37:23** your word says: *The steps of a good man are ordered by the LORD. And he delighteth in his way.*

Lord God, I declare that you have ordered my steps this morning. I delight in your words, and I am receiving your loving kindness, your joy and your peace to lead me today. I believe that you are with me and you are defending me today and always. I believe that you have already cleared the way for me and my family, even before the foundation of the world. O Lord God, help me to take pleasure in you at all times because I am safe and secure in you.

Lord, I am asking you to defeat every plan of the enemies on behalf of everyone, today and always. Please keep us safe at all times. Cover our neighbourhood, our home and family. Lord, please cover our workplace and all our co-workers.

I pray for safety for all the road users, for those who travel on the sea and in the air. I pray for our governments, that they will acknowledge you as the greater leader. I pray for both spiritual and political leaders. Help them to be willing to serve you as Lord and saviour, for without you we can do nothing that is good.

Lord, I increase my faith with confidence that whatever I ask of you this morning according to your will. It shall be granted, in the mighty name of Jesus Christ, I pray.

Amen.

General Morning Prayer - Part 2

HEBREWS 4:16

Let us therefore come boldly to the throne of grace, that we may obtain mercy, and find grace to help in time of need.

GOD of grace, creator of the visible and invisible, I honour and glorify you, for you are the Most High God. Lord, you are the creator of heaven and earth. I bow my knees and I call you Holy, I call you Mighty, I call you the Eternal God, for you alone are Lord over my life.

Father, your throne room is in the heavens but by faith, you have caused me to enter into your throne room every day with thanksgiving and prayers for others and myself. Lord, it is a high calling; it is a glorious calling and opportunity for everyone to come boldly to your throne of grace. Let your living water flow over me and refresh me. I thank you for the call of hope.

Lord, this call is a great privilege for me. I recognised that you are the KING OF KINGS AND THE LORD OF LORDS. Your call is a universal call, and everyone has the same opportunity to come to you. God, I know that I cannot live without your grace and your mercy, so this morning I open up my heart's door to you. I ask that you will fill me up with the power of your wisdom, knowledge and understanding. Fill me up and empower me, dear Lord, with your anointing. Help me to absorb all your principles and all your characteristics. Help me to know the right way to live so that I can receive eternal life from you.

Lord, I am aware that I do not deserve your grace, but you chose me and appointed me for greatness. Merciful God I am conscious that your divine favours have transformed my life. Lord, you have taken away discouragements and you have given me encouragement, you have taken away fears and you have given me confidence, to receive all the benefits of your grace.

I ask that you will help me to see the need of someone today, and I will be willing to help as much as you have directed me to.

Father, I love you with my whole heart, and I want to love your people the way that you want me to love them.

Hear my prayer dear Lord. I ask for your continual grace and your mercy. In the mighty name of Jesus Christ, I pray.

Amen.

Why We Pray - Part 1

THROUGHOUT the Bible, there are many examples of prayer. God designed prayer and He encourages us to pray. When we pray it releases us from our inner pains, it refreshes us and builds up our confidence and relationship with God. We pray because it is one of the most powerful spiritual weapons that God has given us to use to receive help from him.

Prayer is a dialogue, we speak to God and he answers us. Prayer positions us to have a connection with God. Prayer allowed the anointing of God's power to transform us, and helped us to draw strength, courage and healing from him, and so much more.

God has made us in his own image so that we can communicate with him through prayer. God has designed prayer so that we can have intimacy with him. Prayer is a powerful way to worship God. Someone says that prayer is like a master key that opens heaven's door. Prayer is a way of creating an agreement with God that will open doors of opportunities for our lives.

Prayer is not a religion, or made-up words, it is a life of fellowship with God. Prayer is a heavenly treasure that God has given unto us. We can pray and bring down the strongholds of our enemies, and create personal changes in our lives.

Prayer allows us to receive God's favours into our lives and bind up the forces of evil. Prayer is like a powerful spiritual bank account. The more you pray and connect with God, the more interest you gain.

We can receive many things from God when we pray. For example, we can receive benefits such as healing, protection and directions. We can receive physical, mental, emotional and spiritual help from the Lord. Prayer opens the doors to peace of mind, a close relationship with God, blessings in abundance and, most of all, eternal life.

Prayer is a blessed, spiritual virtue of giving and receiving. We give of our prayer, time, money, love, mercy and compassion. We give from all the resources that God has blessed us with, and we receive abundant blessings in good measures from God.

Prayer is like a spiritual blanket that can cover us, shield us and protect us. We give thanks to the God of heaven for the power of prayer and all His blessings.

Jesus Christ was a perfect example of prayer. He prayed all night many times.

Luke 6:12: *And it came to pass in those days, that he went out into a mountain to pray, and continued all night in prayer to God.*

According to **Luke 18:1*:** Jesus teaches us that: *Men ought always to pray, and not to faint.* This means: Do not get discouraged or downhearted, do not give up, but continue to pray.

Matthew 6:6: *But thou, when you prayest, enter into thy closet, and when thou hast shut thy door, pray to thy Father which is in secret, and thy Father which seeth in secret, shall reward thee openly.*

Colossians 4:2: *Continue in prayer, and watch in the same with thanksgiving.*

Romans 12:12: *Rejoice in hope patient in tribulation: continue instant in prayer.*

Mark 11:24: *Therefore, I say unto you what things soever ye desire, when ye pray, believe that ye receive them, and ye shall have them.*

1 John 1:9: *If we confess our sins, he is faithful and just to forgive us our sins, and to cleanse us from all unrighteousness.*

Philippians 4:6: *Be careful (anxious) for nothing; but in everything by prayer and supplication with thanksgiving let, your requests be made known unto God.*

*Full scripture: Luke 18:1 [Bible Citations: pg 206]

Why We Pray - Part 2

We pray because prayer is one of the highest form of worship. Prayer brings us into a closer relationship with God, it builds up our confidence in him and we receive revelations.

Prayer allows us to hear the voice of God in many different ways, as He speaks to reassure us.

Prayer is one source of the life giving stream that gives inner healing and inner comfort.

In **Matthew 7:7:** Jesus said: *Ask, and it shall be given you; seek, and ye shall find; knock, and it shall be opened unto you.*

Prayer is designed for us to give glory, honour and respect to the Lord Jesus Christ.

Prayer creates an atmosphere in which we can prosper and be in good health.

Prayer is a gateway to worship God, as we acknowledge him as our Lord, saviour, creator and redeemer.

Prayer allows our faith to increase and grow. It empowers us to overcome barriers and break down strongholds that may want to come to hold us captive.

When we pray, God keeps an accurate record of our prayer.

When we pray we are demonstrating our love for God and towards others.

When we pray we do not know how long we will have to wait for God to answer our prayers, but we must believe that God is able, and well capable to hear and answer our prayers in His own time.

We should always have an attitude of humility, willingness and patience, to wait with thanksgiving and confidence that God will hear and answer our prayers.

We should pray in faith and believe that God will act on our behalf according to his will.

We should pray the word of God, the word of God has power to increase, it is a living seed, it is active, always doing something for us. **Psalm 119:11:** *Thy word have I hid in my heart that I might not sin against thee.*

Praying the word of God has power to transform us; it has power to cleanse us to keep us pure. **Psalm 119:9:** *Wherewithal, shall a young man cleans his ways? by taking heed thereto the word of God.*

According to **Matthew 6: 9-15**, Jesus teaches His disciples how to pray, and how to receive.

Look at **14-15**: *[14] For if we forgive men their trespasses, your heavenly Father will also forgive you: [15] But if ye forgive not men their trespasses, neither will your Father forgive your trespasses.*

***Forgiveness* is a powerful key that is very important to our prayer life, for us to get the right result from the Lord.**

Prayer for Peace

IT IS TIME TO PRAY | 31

Pray for the peace of Jerusalem

PSALM 122:6

Pray for the peace of Jerusalem: they shall prosper that love thee.

LORD God of Abraham, Isaac and Jacob, you are the God who stretched out the heavens like a curtain. I give thanks to your holy, exalted name. I thank you that you are the sovereign Lord. You are the almighty God. You are the God who never changes and the God who never fails. You are the omnipresent God, the omniscient God, and the omnipotent God. You are the conquering lion of the tribe of Judah. Today I call upon your name for the peace of Jerusalem, the place where you chose to put your name.

Lord, I ask that you silence, crush and destroy the plans of the enemies concerning Israel. Lord God, in **Psalm 122:6** you have asked us to pray for the peace of Jerusalem. I pray in obedience for your perfect peace to abide with your people, for you are the Prince of peace.

Lord, according to **Isaiah 54:17.** I ask that no weapon that is formed against your people shall prosper or succeed, and every tongue that rises up against them in judgment shall be condemned. Lord Jesus, I declare your delivering blood, your sustaining blood over the people of Israel. Wherever in the world they may be O Lord, I ask that you will protect them, and keep them from all harm and danger.

Lord God Almighty, we ask that you will be a stronghold for them in times of trouble and in times of danger. Lord, help them to depend on you for their shield and their defence. Be a bulwark of protection around them O Lord. Merciful God, when the enemies surround them like a flood, I ask that you, O Lord, will lift up a standard and defeat their enemies.

Almighty God, gracious God, you are the sovereign Lord; I humbly call upon your name, Lord Jesus, for help. I declare your blessings upon the children of Israel continually. O God, in **Genesis 12:3*:** you have promised that you will bless those that bless Israel, and you will curse those that curse them.

As the walls surround Jerusalem, so let the power of your grace surround your people continually. Father let the abiding fragrance and the aroma of your love, continue to sustain and strengthen Israel.

Mighty God, according to **Ephesians 3:20.** I believe that you are able to do exceedingly, abundantly, above all that we can ask or think. According to your power that is working in the lives of your people. Lord please build a fire wall around your people and protect them from evil.

Most of all Lord, I ask that Israel will acknowledge you as their Lord and Saviour. Lord, please help them to be committed to serve you in holiness and humility.

Gracious God, I thank you for releasing your blessings upon your people, as they come in agreement in prayer and receive your blessings in the mighty name of Jesus Christ. Shalom.

Amen.

*Full scripture: Genesis 12: 3 [Bible Citations: pg 206]

Prayer of Thanksgiving for God's grace

GOD'S grace gives us His unmerited favour to receive salvation. We cannot work for grace.
God has been given us all good things that we did not deserve.
God's grace gives us favours out of the treasure of His Divine love.
God is daily supplying all our needs according to His divine will.

Titus 2:11-14
[11] *For the grace of God that brings salvation hath appeared to all men.*
[12] *Teaching us that, denying ungodliness and worldly lusts, we should live soberly, righteously and godly, in this present world.*
[13] *Looking for that blessed hope, and glorious appearing of the great God and our Saviour Jesus Christ.*
[14] *Who gave himself for us, that he might redeem us from all iniquity, and purify unto himself a peculiar people, zealous of good works.*

LORD, I thank you that your grace will always show up for me. Eternal God, your love, your grace, and your mercy have given me life. You came down from heaven to earth to rescue me from the powers of darkness when I could not help myself. Lord, you have opened the door of deliverance for me when I was in captivity by sin.

Father, even though many times I forget to say thanks. Sovereign Lord, right now I want to say thanks to you for all that you have done for me.

This morning I rise from by bed, to thank you for your loving kindness, you have given me a life beyond the grave. Today I live because of you O Lord. I am willing to deny ungodliness and worldly lusts. I am determined to live in sobriety and righteousness to receive the blessed hope of eternal life.

Mighty God, I thank you for your compassionate love that surrounds me day by day. Your plan of salvation has delivered me from the kingdom of darkness, and you have transferred me into the kingdom of light. This morning I open the treasure box of your grace and receive your healing power to strengthen and comfort me. Lord, you have made me to be a channel of blessing to do good work for you.

Merciful God because of your grace, I have victory over the plans of the enemies. Your divine blood on the cross of Calvary has given me salvation and eternal life. I thank you for crushing the head of Satan and breaking down his kingdom, so that I can have access to your kingdom.

Merciful God, your grace gave me great riches, your grace has closed the gates of hell and open the gates of heaven for me. Your grace brought healing and deliverance to me. Your grace has removed spiritual blindness and has opened my eyes to the truth of your word.

I have denied un-godliness and worldly lust to walk with you and to live with you. Lord, I give you thanks, and I will show my appreciation to you at all times.

Help me always to acknowledge that your presence is with me. Holy Father, I ask that you hear and answer my prayers of faith in the name of Jesus, I pray.

Amen.

Thanksgiving for My Personal Connection to God

JOHN 8:32

And ye shall know the truth, and the truth shall make you free.

O, LORD my God, how excellent is your name in all the earth. The heavens and the earth bow down before you. The heavens and the earth exalt your holy name. I thank you God, that you are my rock, my strength and my high tower. I thank you God that you have delivered me from the hands of the enemies. I thank you Lord Jesus, that you have removed me from the kingdom of separation, to the kingdom of unity and relationship with you.

Lord according to *John 8:32* I declare your truth over my life. Lord, I am passionate to know the truth about you. I am seeking to know more about you. I do not want to be in the darkness.

Today I am pursuing after you, for you are the Way the Truth and the Life. Lord, only you can make me free, only you can make me clean, only you can make me healthy and strong.

O God of grace, I seek to find safety and security in you alone. I seek to find comfort and strength in you alone. Mighty God, please give me the confidence to trust in you all the days of my life.

Gracious and sovereign God, by faith I declare that you have given me good health. I declare that I am well and vibrant, I am restored,

I am watered, and I am connected to you. I am meditating on your words day and night. According to *Psalm 1:3**: I am producing fruit in its season, because you have planted me by the rivers of water. Lord, my leaves shall not whither and whatsoever I do shall always prosper. Merciful God, I am convinced that every day you are preparing me for greatness. I am producing good and desirable fruits in the mighty name of Jesus Christ, hallelujah.

Father, I declare that according to *Jude: 24-25**: you are able to keep me from falling. You are able to present me without fault before the presence of your glory with exceeding joy. For you are the only wise God my saviour. To your name be majesty, dominion and power both now and forever. Hallelujah to Jesus.

Lord Jesus, you have promised that if I abide in you. According to *John 15:7**: and allow your words to abide in me, Lord, you have promised that I can ask for what I need, and you will give it to me. Lord, please remind me that you have promised to supply all my needs. Mighty God, I speak to the mountain of sickness, fear, doubts and all that stand in my way. I command them to get out of my way by the anointing power of Jesus Christ. Lord, I put my trust in you to perform and accomplish that which I ask in the Mighty name of Jesus Christ. Praise God, praise God.

O Lord God, I thank you for hearing and answering my prayers of faith. In the mighty name of Jesus Christ of Nazareth, I pray.

Amen.

*Full scripture: Psalm 1:3, Jude: 24-25, John 15: 7 [Bible Citations: pg 207]

Prayer for my Healing - Part 1

ROMANS 15:13

And now the God of hope fill you with all joy, and peace in believing that ye may abound in hope, through the power of the Holy Ghost.

This morning I rise to praise the Holy, Exalted name of Jesus Christ. I thank you that you have won the victory at the cross of Calvary for my healing. Lord according to **Romans 15:13** my hope is in you alone, Lord; I believe that you are capable to heal me, and fill me with joy through the power of your Holy Spirit.

You have given me the privilege to come to you by faith right now, to receive my healing. Lord, today I declare that your healing blood is running through my veins, at this very minute, and you are performing healing in my body. I declare that Jehovah Rapha is healing me right now. I receive your words according to **Psalm 107:20*:** that you have sent your words to heal all my disease and you have delivered me from destructions. Hallelujah.

Father, you are the great physician and there is no sickness or disease that you cannot heal nor cure. You are my healer and my deliverer; you are my way-maker and the source of my healing. Lord you are the lifter of my head.

Lord according to **Isaiah 53:5*:** I understand that you were wounded for my transgression, you were bruised for my inequity, the chastisement of my peace was upon you and by your stripes (beatings), I am healed. I receive my healing right now in the mighty name of Jesus Christ.

Mighty God, I declare **3 John 1:2** over my life: *Beloved, I wish above all things that thou mayest prosper and be in health, even as thy soul prospereth.* Lord, I receive and embrace this word in my mind in my body and in my spirit. I shall prosper and be in good health even as my soul prospers.

I declare that I shall live pain free, sickness free and stress free in the mighty name of Jesus. For I am appointed and anointed for your service, my spirit shall dominate my body to function just as you designed it to. I declare that my mind is healed, my brain cells are healed in the mighty name of Jesus. I refuse memory loss or any form of confusion to enter my brain. I declare wellness in the name of Jesus Christ.

I speak with stability and consciousness in the mighty name of Jesus.

Amen.

*Full scripture: Psalm 107:20, Isaiah 53:5 [Bible Citations: pg 207]

Prayer for my Healing - Part 2

PHILIPPIANS 1:6

Being confident of this very thing, that he which hath began a good work in you will perform it until the day of Jesus Christ.

FATHER God, according to **Philippians 1:6*:** I have confidence that you have begun a good work in me. You are able to perform it. Lord you are able to accomplish it until the day of Jesus Christ. Mighty God I declare that I have trust in your word and your word is performing a good work in me.

Today I speak to my eyes, my ears and my mouth to be healed. I command my teeth, my tongue and my nose to be healed in the mighty name of Jesus Christ.

I declare that my throat, my heart and my lungs are healed. My liver, my kidneys, my gall bladder and my spleen are healed in the mighty name of Jesus Christ. I speak to my pancreas and to every blood vessel to line up with the word of God and be healed in the name of Jesus.

I speak to my bladder and my bone marrow, my breast, my stomach and all the intestines in my body to be healed in the mighty name of Jesus. I command every bone, every muscle and joint in my body to be healed, and every other tissue of my body, from the crown of my head to the soles of my feet I declare healing in the mighty, exalted name of Jesus Christ.

Lord, you are EL Shaddai.
The Lord God Almighty.

You are El Elyon.
The Most High God.

You are Jehovah Nissi.
The Lord My Banner.

You are Jehovah Rapha.
The Lord That Heals.

Almighty God, sovereign God, by faith, I speak healing to every organ that is in my body to function the way God has designed it to function. In the mighty name of Jesus Christ

Lord, I believe that you are in your word, and your word is working in me. I have all faith and confidence that your healing power is taking place in my body right now. Lord, I believe that I am set free from the curse of sin, sickness, disease and all different types of discomfort that may want to attack my body. I declare the healing power of the Lord Jesus Christ to take control over my body right now, in the mighty name of Jesus.

Lord, by faith I have received my miracle healing today through the mighty name of Jesus Christ of Nazareth, hallelujah, praise God. Praise God. Thank you Lord, for hearing and answering my prayers. In the mighty name of Jesus Christ, I pray. Hallelujah.

Amen.

*Full scripture: Philippians 1: 6 [Bible Citations: pg 207]

Personal Prayer - Part 1

PSALM 5:3

*My voice shalt thou hear in the morning, O LORD;
in the morning will I direct my prayer unto thee,
and will look up.*

ETERNAL God, I worship and adore your Holy exalted name. I give thanks to you for this holy day. It is a day of thanksgiving and praise to your name. Lord, I am conscious that it is also a day of challenges. Today I declare that it is a day of new beginning for my healing. Lord, as I rise this morning I ask you to go before me and clear the way for me and everyone.

Lord according to **Psalm 5:3**, I have committed in my heart to direct my prayer request unto you in the mornings. I look up to you diligently this morning and I wait in expectation to receive blessings from you.

Lord just like David was committed to pray to you in the morning, so I am determined to commit and direct my prayer to you. I believe that you are able and capable to make my way blessed and prosperous every day.

Lord, I have purpose in my heart that I will receive the fragrance of your loving kindness to talk with you every morning. Father, I will build my relationship with you, as I wake out of sleep. I give you honour; I give you all the praise, I will rejoice in you. I appreciate you, O Lord God. Father this morning, I am committed to have a new mind to worship you, to glorify your Holy exalted name. Lord, you are a good God to me.

I thank you that you have allowed your Holy Spirit to live inside of me. Lord, help me to love people the same way that you have loved me. Help me to be merciful and compassionate to your people, for we are very important to you.

This morning I ask that your peace will continue to cover me through the storms of life, for only in you I am safe, only in you I am secure, only in you I find peace. Lord, please cover me when I am hurting, cover me when I am sad, cover me when no one seems to care. Cover me, Lord, when life seems hopeless; cover me when my faith is weak. Cover my mind dear Lord, let not the enemies triumph over me.

Lord, I thank you so much that I can have a relationship with you. Although you are the King of Kings and the Lord of Lords, you chose to love me. Lord, I thank you for the daily protection and provisions that you have given to me, so that I can have a hope beyond the grave. Lord, I thank you for helping me to understand that you are the one who is loading me daily with benefits.

O Lord God Almighty, I love you, and my desire is to please you in everything.

O Lord, please help me to trust you in everything. I ask your mercy in the name of Jesus.

Amen.

Personal Prayer - Part 2

HEBREWS 4:16

Let us therefore come boldly unto the throne of grace, that we may obtain mercy, and find grace to help in time of need.

GOD of grace, I thank you for this welcome call of your grace. This call is a great opportunity for me and for everyone who is willing to accept it. You have called me to come boldly to your throne room, so that I can receive mercy and grace to help me even in these troubled times.

Lord, as I enter into your throne room this morning, I bow down before you, because I am in need of your help in my everyday life.

O Lord God Almighty, I vow to praise you, I vow to honour you. Lord you have chosen to reveal your holy, exalted name to me. I thank you that your Divine love, you have granted me favours, and you have surrounded me daily so that I can receive benefits both from you and from man. Father because of your love for me, I am now receiving confidence from you to speak your word over my life and over my family's life.

According to *2 Corinthians 10:4* your words declare that: *For the weapons of our warfare are not carnal, but mighty through God to the pulling down of strongholds.* Lord, right now I am drawing spiritual strength and spiritual energy from you. Lord by your power, you are helping me to pull down every stronghold of the enemy. Lord Jesus, by the power of your name I cancel every assignment of the enemy. I use the weapons of prayer and fasting to break down every wall of the enemy. In the mighty name of Jesus Christ.

Lord, you have given me the authority and spiritual power to use these powerful weapons to cancel, to uproot and destroy every seed that is sown by the enemies to stop my spiritual growth.

Lord, you have given me victory by removing the spirit of fear, doubt, confusion, and heaviness to reverse every plan and evert tricks of the wicked one. Lord, you have replaced your anointing peace and boldness inside me to help me to overcome. Lord, you have promised that you will keep me in your perfect peace if my mind is always thinking about you. I am willing to think about you at all times. Mighty God, right now, I am dwelling in a place of peace in Jesus name.

My desire, by your divine grace, is to submit my life to your will at all times. I am willing to serve you in worship, in holiness and in honour, all the days of my life.

O Lord God, please help me to allow you to work through my life, so that your name will be glorify. In the name of Jesus, I pray.

Amen.

Prayer for Spiritual Leaders - Part 1

ISAIAH 55:10-11

¹⁰ For as the rain cometh down, and the snow from heaven, and returneth not thither, but watereth the earth, and maketh it bring forth and bud, that it may give seed to the sower, and bread to the eater: ¹¹ So shall my word be that goeth forth out of my mouth: It shall not return to me void, but it shall accomplish that which I please, and it shall prosper in the thing whereto I send it.

WONDERFUL, merciful Saviour, Mighty God of the universe, I give you thanks for your loving kindness. I thank you, O Lord, because you are the head of the church. Lord, only you have the authority and power to position your church.

Lord, according to *Isaiah 55:10-11* you speak about the firmness of your **WORD**. Lord, I have confidence that your word is a living organism. Your word is active. Your word brings creation into being.

Your word will always be effective to accomplish that which you declared it to do because there is power in your **WORD**. Lord, there is power in your word to heal the sick, to save souls and to restore broken lives. I pray that all spiritual leaders will SPEAK your word just as you command them to do.

Holy Father, please help all spiritual leaders to understand that the church is your domain, and you are Lord and King over your church. Merciful Father, please help your leaders to follow your instructions and your directions in obedience. According to ***Ephesians 4:11-12:*** *¹¹And he gave some apostles; and some, prophets; and some, evangelists; and some, pastors and teachers. ¹²For the perfecting of the saints, for the work of the ministry, for the edifying of the body of Christ.* Lord, these verses declared that you appoint leaders, and gave spiritual gifts to them, to teach and to preach your word.

Lord, I pray for your ministering servants, all the Bishops, Apostles, Pastors, Overseers and Evangelists. I pray for all your Ministers, Missionaries, Deacons, and all those that you have called to minister for you. Father, I ask that they will consciously consider their responsibilities and purpose as leaders. Help them never to see their titles so great that they forget their purpose and their responsibilities towards you and your people.

Lord, I pray that you will help them to be good leaders and good shepherds over the flock. Lord, please help them to be willing, dedicated and committed to the positions that you have placed upon their lives for your glory.

Lord, I thank you that according to ***Matthew 16:18*** you declare that you will build your church and the gates of hell shall not prevail against it. Lord, you have given me the confidence to know that, as long as I am a part of your church, I am safe and I am secured. I am in a place of divine safety and protection because I am in you and you are in me.

Lord, I give thanks to you for hearing and answering my prayers of faith. In the mighty name of Jesus, I pray.

Amen.

Prayer for Spiritual Leaders - Part 2

PSALM 37:37

Mark the perfect man, and behold the upright: for the end of that man is peace.

MERCIFUL, wonderful Saviour, today I honour your holy, exalted name. I give thanks to you for your holiness, your grace, your everlasting mercies and your compassionate love.

Lord, I thank you for all spiritual leaders. I pray that they will allow your Holy Spirit to lead them as they minister for you. Lord God, I pray that you will help them to live in your peace and uprightness. I pray against every attack of the enemies. Lord, I pray against every deceiving spirit, every lying and contrary spirit that may rise up against your spiritual leaders to bring fear upon them.

Mighty God, I pray for boldness and confidence, I pray that they will speak your words with power and authority, so that souls can be changed from an old lifestyle to a new lifestyle in you, and that souls will transform from the kingdom of darkness to the kingdom of light so that your name will be glorified.

Holy Father, I pray for inspiration and revelations for your ministers. Help them to preach your words effectively by the anointing of your Holy Spirit. O Lord, I pray that your leaders will not be spiritually blind, but they will be alert and watchful. Help them to keep their focus and be observant as good shepherds. O

God, please anoint them to be humble and willing to serve you freely. Help them to follow godly principles and godly character so that your name will be glorified at all times.

Father, help them to always be willing and ready to serve the needy, not only with the spiritual food but also with the natural food. Lord, as they listen to the cries of your people, give them a compassionate heart to seek out ways in which they can help the needy. Lord, help them to be honest in making decisions and not to be partial or oppressive. Holy Father, help them to remember the elderly, especially those of the body of Christ.

According to *1 Peter 5:2-4**: you have called upon spiritual leaders to feed your people with your word, not by constraint or for filthy lucre (money), but to serve with the right attitude and for the right purpose, for you are the rewarder.

Father God, I pray that our spiritual leaders will be of a good example in their homes, in their communities, at their workplaces and among the body of Christ. Lord, help them to be aware that their lives are an open book to the world.

Eternal God, please anoint your leaders afresh for service. I thank you for hearing and answering my prayer of faith. In the Holy name of Jesus Christ, I pray.

Amen.

*Full scripture: 1 Peter 5: 2-4 [Bible Citations: pg 207]

Prayer for the Government - Part 1

PSALM 51:6

Behold thou desirest truth in the inward parts: and in the hidden part thou shall make me to know wisdom.

HOLY Father, God of heaven, I give glory, honour and praise to your name, because of who you are. Lord Jesus, I thank you that when you came to earth you demonstrated true leadership and true government to the inhabitants of the earth.

Lord, in *1 Timothy 2:1**: you have reminded us to pray for all those who are in authority, that they will be godly and honest. Today I pray for the government that they will live in obedience to your word, so that they will obtain wisdom to lead effectively.

Lord, I pray for the human government, that they will follow your examples so that they can be good and wise leaders. Help them to make wise decisions so that the people will not suffer because of their wrong or unwise decisions. Help them never to be abusive, oppressive or selfish.

Gracious God, today I pray for all those who are in leadership positions. I pray for the Prime Minister, the President, and other heads of government across the globe, as well as all the government supporters that serve your people. Lord, I ask for your divine presence to be with them as they serve. They will not only see it as a job, but they will serve in reverence to you. Help all leaders to know that you are the greater ruler and leader over them.

Lord I pray that you will help leaders to know that it is impossible for their leadership to be effective, unless they are following your instructions. Help them not to think of themselves more highly than they actually are. Please help all leaders to be humble. Lord, help them to demonstrate good understanding for human needs, and seek to help in whatever way they can.

Father, I thank you for hearing and answering my prayer. In the name of Jesus, I pray.

Amen.

*Full scripture: 1 Timothy 2: 1 [Bible Citations: pg 208]

Prayer for the Government - Part 2

PROVERBS 1:7

The fear of the LORD is the beginning of knowledge: but fools despise wisdom and instruction.

O LORD, creator of heaven and earth, I look to you on behalf of those who serve in the government because good leadership are very important to you and to your people.

Lord, help them to do what is right in your sight. Help them to be wise people of good integrity to represent you and the country.

Help them to consult you first so that they can be honest when making decisions. Lord, please give our leaders knowledge to take instructions, to know that they cannot serve the country effectively without your help, for without your help the people will suffer under their leadership.

Lord, in **Psalm 33:12** your words declare: *Blessed is the nation whose God is the LORD: and the people whom he hath chosen for his own inheritance.* Lord, only you can declare blessings upon a nation. A people that recognise, respect and honour you as the true God of heaven; they will receive the true inheritance from you.

Holy Father, may you help our government to observe your words and to live by them, so that this world can be a better place to live. Help them to demonstrate righteous judgements, teach them to use wisdom, knowledge and understanding. O gracious Lord, please give them the ability to serve in humility and honesty.

Sovereign Lord, today I declare blessing upon the government.

I declare protection and provision upon them.

I declare wisdom knowledge and understanding upon them.

I declare your peace and assurance upon them.

I denounce fear and I ask for confidence and boldness for all leaders.

Mighty God, I know that it is hard to rule our house, and I am conscious that it is harder to rule a country.

Father I ask for blessings for our leaders and for all people, because we all need your help. Lord, I honour and respect you. I ask for your mercies in the name of Jesus.

Amen.

Prayer for Young Godly Men Who Are Seeking a Wife

EPHESIANS 5:25

Husbands, love your wives, even as Christ also loved the church, and gave himself for it.

PROVERBS 18:22

Whoso findeth a wife findeth a good thing, and obtaineth favour of the LORD.

Let us Pray

BLESSED Holy Spirit, I give glory, honour and praise to your holy exalted name. I thank you for your divine plan for humanity.

Lord, you designed man in a special unique way to function according to your plans. You provided the organs and reproductive systems to produce life. Lord, you know that a man on his own cannot fulfil this purpose without a wife. You provided women so that your will can be accomplished.

Lord, at this time I am asking you to provide a wife for the young men, that are of age who and are seeking a long-life relationship. Father, also help them to pray and ask you to help them to make the right and suitable choice, so that your purpose can be fulfilled in their lives.

Great God of heaven, when you have fulfilled this petition, please teach the young men how to love their wives, how to place values on them, how to see their wives as a blessing and know that they have obtained favour from you, according to **Proverbs 18:22.** I pray that the young men will know how to lead their families to you in righteousness, just as you have commanded them to do.

Mighty God, I ask that you will anoint the young men with your Holy Spirit, Lord, please do a transition in their lives, so that they will be able to produce godly principles and godly characters. Help them to be honest and respectful to their wives at all times. Lord, help them to set a good example in their home, in the church and in their community.

O Lord, I ask for a special blessing and a special anointing on the young men that their lives will be set apart for your service.

O God, please use them for your glory, that they will also be a blessing and a good example to other young men. Father, I ask that you will hear my prayer. In the name of Jesus, I pray.

Amen.

Prayer for Young Women in General

LUKE 1:42

And she spake out with a loud voice, and said, Blessed art thou among woman and blessed is the fruit of thy womb.

FATHER, in the name of Jesus, I give you thanks, I give you the honour and I give you the highest praise. Hallelujah.

I bow down and worship you; I honour and glorify you, for you alone are worthy. Lord, I ask that your Holy Spirit will do a transition in the lives of young women.

Lord, by faith I declare **Luke 1:42** over young women lives, that just like Elisabeth prophesied blessings upon Mary, so I declare blessings upon the lives of our young women. Lord, I speak strength and courage into their innermost being. Lord, I speak into the hearts of our young women that they will make themselves available for your service just like the godly women.

Deliver them from the forces of darkness and use them for your glory. Lord, I declare your Holy presence will transform young women that they will place values upon their lives. Merciful Father, help them to aspire to be godly women with godly characters. Father, plant a holy seed in young women as you did to Mary, Ruth and Elisabeth. Lord, please grant the young women wisdom like Esther. She was willing to fast and pray for her people, to save them from the evil hands of the wicked. Lord, I pray that the young women will take position in spiritual battle just like Deborah, so that they can fulfil their full potential. Lord please allow young women to aspire for greatness.

Today I declare the presence of God over every young woman. The Spirit of God will direct, strengthen and sustain you in the name of Jesus. The face of God shine upon you. The hand of God fight for you and defend you. The power and wisdom of God guide and protect you in the mighty name of Jesus Christ.

I declare that the eyes of God watch over you and your family. The hands of God carry you. The peace of God embrace and preserve you. The goodness and mercies of God surround you and console you and your family in the name of Jesus. The grace of God speak for you and through you. The angels of God surround you and your family in the mighty name of Jesus Christ of Nazareth.

Lord, I speak wisdom, knowledge and understanding to all young woman to have a desire to read your words. Lord please let your words transform them, and liberate them, to be victorious over the world and its pleasures.

Holy God, please help the young women, so that they will be able to testify about you and their testimony will be able to transform lives. Help them to be a shining light in this dark world, so that their Christ-like lives will open the door for souls to receive salvation.

Lord, I thank you for hearing and answering my prayer of faith. In the mighty name of Jesus, I pray.

Amen.

Prayer for Young Men in General - Part 1

1 JOHN 2:14

I have written unto you, young men, because ye are strong, and the word of God abideth in you, and ye have overcome the wicked one.

LORD, you have called upon the young men because they are strong. Merciful Father, today I give you thanks for all young men, that you will help them as they travel on life's journey. Their physical strength may fail, Father, but I pray that you will empower them with both physical and spiritual strength for your glory.

O God, life is not always easy, many times life is a struggle, and many young men find it very difficult to cope. O Lord, when you designed humanity, you had a purpose and a plan for each one of us. In **Jeremiah 29:11*:** you told him that you know the thoughts that you think towards him, thoughts of peace and not evil, to give him an expected end.

Lord, you are our maker and life giver. Almighty God, we cannot live without you, and we cannot survive without you. Just like Jeremiah, you also have a plan for all young men.

Today I am presenting the young men into your divine care. I ask that you will save them and allow them to submit to your rule, so that they will be able to perform the duties that you have designed for their lives. Lord, I ask that you will provide for the young men, protect them from harm and danger. O Lord, you are their hiding place. O Lord, help them to run to you in times of brokenness and despair, in times when darkness surrounds them. Lord, please water them, when it seems as if there is no hope. Help them to find assurance in you, help them to know that you care for them. Help them to be humble and know that you are the Lord their God and they are in a winning position.

Lord, I ask that you will grant the young men all the godly principles and godly character that they need, so that they will be able to fulfil their purpose. I ask that you will educate them and provide good jobs for them. Mighty God, allow the power of your Holy Spirit to transform the young men and allow them to look beyond the naturalness of life. Help the young men not only to see with their natural eyes, but through the eyes of your Holy Spirit.

O God, reveal yourself to the young men in a very special way for your glory. In Jesus name, I pray.

Amen.

*Full scripture: Jeremiah 29: 11 [Bible Citations: pg 208]

Prayer for Young Men in General - Part 2

ISAIAH 55: 6-7

⁶ Seek ye the LORD while ye may be found, call ye upon him while he is near: ⁷ Let the wicked forsake is way, and the unrighteous man his thoughts: and let him return unto the LORD, and he will have mercy upon him; and to our God, for he will abundantly pardon.

FATHER, in the name of Jesus, I exalt your Holy name, Lord your name is above every other name, for at your name **JESUS** every knee shall bow, of things in heaven, of things in earth and things under the earth. And every tongue shall confess the Jesus Christ is Lord. **(Philippians 2:10-11)**

I come to you on behalf of the young men. Lord I declare **Isaiah 55:6-7** over their lives that they will seek you; that they will call upon you, and turn to you because you will pardon them, you will have mercy on them, you will deliver them and save them from the fire of hell.

O Lord, I thank you that you have given me the access, and the privileges. I thank you for the opportunity to come to you in prayer. I bring the young men to you dear Lord, I bring their burdens and their cares to you, for only you are able to help them.

O Lord, I ask that you will supply the young men with wisdom, knowledge and understanding, just like you gave to King Solomon, so that they will be able and willing to perform your work as you daily support them. Please take away weakness from the young men, O Lord, and replace it with spiritual, physical and emotional strength. Help them to have respect for you and for each other. Take away discouragement and replace it with encouragement. Lord, please take away failures and disappointments and replace them with confidence to trust in you. Father, please give the young men a spiritual focus; please give them a desire to be your willing vessels.

Lord, remember those who are behind bars, I ask you for grace. Grant them favours. O Mighty God, please deliver them from the evil of sin. Lord Jesus, please set them free from the hands of the enemy and of the deception of sin. Help them to have a change of mind from the affairs of this world and encourage them to call upon you for help.

By faith I call the young men from behind bars, I call them to a changed life in you, Christ Jesus. I call the young men from a life of hopelessness to a life of hope in the mighty name of Jesus. Lord. You can use them for your purpose.

Mighty God, I ask that you will hear and answer my prayer of faith. In the exalted name of Jesus, I pray.

Amen.

Prayer for Godly Young Women Who Desire to Be Married

LUKE 1:30

And the angel said unto her, Fear not Mary; for thou hast found favour with God.

LORD GOD of the universe, creator of all things, Lord, you see everything and you know everything. Holy Father, when you designed woman, you carefully designed her for your purpose.

Lord, you designed her with all the necessary requirements to bring life into the world. You have equipped her with the abilities to be affectionate, loving, caring and kind. You gave her desires and needs for a husband, so as she lives for you, her life can fulfil your plans.

Father it is important for us to know that favours comes from you, and just like you granted favour to Mary so I ask that you will grant favour to all godly women who are desirous to get married.

Lord, I ask that you will provide a godly man that will love her and care for her. A man that will respect her and value her life. A man that will embrace her and show affection to her. Lord, please select an honest and generous man that will demonstrate godly principles and godly characteristics. Gracious Father, you designed a man and a woman to become a union of husband and wife so that they can enjoy life together and to be fruitful by producing children for your glory. Lord, even in difficult situations, let them be willing to discuss matters and pray about the issues.

Father, I ask that a wife will love and respect her husband. She will care for her children. Lord, teach her how to be a good home keeper. Lord, please teach her how to be a godly and a praying wife and mother. Help her to be a true worshipper, one that loves you and is willing to depend on you in everything. Lord, please help her to demonstrate godly principles, to be generous and willing to help where there is a need, so that she will always find favour with God and man. Lord, if the union has any stepchildren, please allow both parents to give the same treatment to each of them and not to be partial. Help the parents not to draw lines to divide their home, for such actions will open doors for the devil to enter and break up their relationship.

Holy God, I commit this prayer to you by faith. Thank you for hearing and answering my prayer in the name of Jesus I pray.

Amen.

Prayer for My Community

EZEKIEL 11:19

And I will give them one heart, and I will put a new spirit within you; and I will take the stony heart out of your flesh, and will give them a heart of flesh.

O Lord, how excellent is your name in all the earth. I exalt you and magnify your name. Mighty God, I believe that if there is only one person in this community that is praying, you can save the city, for you will show kindness and mercy. Lord, help us as a community to pray continually for you are a God of favours.

Mighty God, just as you promised Israel a new heart. I pray that the inhabitancies of our community will receive a new heart from you. Merciful Father, if the heart of the people is corrupted then the community will be open to all kind of evil works. So Lord, I pray that you will take out the stony heart and insert a heart of flesh, that will be filled with love mercy and compassion.

Lord, today I declare safety for the community where I live. I pray for provisions and protection. O Lord, please allow everyone to show duty of care. Help us to share with each other. Help us to demonstrate love towards each other in a genuine way. Father, help us to be our brother's keeper, to treat each other as human beings. Lord, teach us how to deal with matters in a responsible and peaceful way, so that your grace and mercy can be maintain in our community.

Father, I ask that you will help me to be the guard in my community so that I can identify the needs of the people, especially the elders and the children, so that no one will go hungry and that the surrounding environment will be safe. Lord, most of all I pray that my community will acknowledge you as the true and living God. Help everyone to come to you in repentance.

O Lord, I am a resident in this community, you have given me the authority to speak against the spirit of darkness that may try to come into our community. Please help us to break free from every bad habit, every yoke and bondage.

Lord, please take authority against every spiritual attack of the enemies. I speak healing in every household in this community. I speak protection from thieves and wrong doers. I speak against fire and from virus. I speak safety for the children and the elderly. Lord, I speak good health from sickness, disease, bacteria, infection and all other destructive elements, that may want to cut lives short.

Lord, I come in agreement with prayer for all residents, that we will all call upon your holy name for the protection of our community. Father we thank you, we believe that this community is safe and protect by the blood of Jesus Christ.

Thank you for your mercies in this community. In the mighty name of Jesus, I pray.

Amen.

Prayer for My Healing

ISAIAH 41:13*

For I the Lord thy God will hold thy right hand, saying unto thee Fear not I will help thee.

FATHER in heaven, I bow down and worship you O Lord, I give honour to your Holy, Exalted name. Lord, I believe that you are my healer and you have given unto me the access to come into your throne room to make my petition know unto you. Lord, I am confident to declare *Isaiah 41:13* over my life. I believe that you are holding me and reassuring and helping me.

Lord, this morning I come to you with pains, sorrow, discomforts and burdens. Father, your will is that I should be in good health, so today I thank you that your perfect will is embracing me with good health.

Holy Father, your word says, "**By your stripes I am healed**". Lord, I accept your words to be true. For this reason, I declare healing in my body from the crown of my head to the soles of my feet.

There shall be no diabetes or high blood pressure come near my body, for my body is the temple of the living God. I command every memory cell and every brain cell to line up with the word of God. I command every pain and every discomfort to leave my body. Lord, you have given me the authority to command healing to my body. I declare my blood vessels are healed; my joints and muscles are healed in the name of Jesus. O Lord, I thank you that you have sent your word to heal me. You gave me your word to cancel every form of sickness and every form of disease from my body.

Lord, today I declare that I am now living pain free; I am now living in victory. Thank you, Lord, that I can now live a healthy life because of your divine healing blood.

Lord, I thank you for your healing power that you have performed upon my body. In Jesus name, I pray.

Amen

HEALING SCRIPTURES

Psalm 41:4*: *I said, LORD be merciful unto me: heal my soul for I have sinned against thee.*

Isaiah 41:10* Fear thou not; for I am with thee...

Jeremiah 17:14*: Heal me, O LORD, and I shall be healed...

Jeremiah 30:17*: For I will restore health unto thee, and I will heal thee...

Mark 5:34*: And he said unto her, Daughter, they faith hath made thee whole...

Philippians 4:19*: But my God shall supply all your need...

Revelations 21:4*: And God shall wipe away all tears from their eyes...

*Full Scriptures: Psalm 41: 4, Isaiah 41:10, Jeremiah 17:14, Jeremiah 30: 17, Mark 5: 34. Philippians 4: 19 [Bible Citations: pg 208], Revelations 21: 4 [Bible Citations: pg 209]

Prayer for the Bereaved

HEBREWS 9: 27

And as it is appointed unto men once to die, but after this the judgment.

O LORD, I give thanks and praise to you for this precious gift of life that you have lent to me. Lord, I thank you that you are the life giver and you know the measure of my days. Holy Father, when you take back life from our loved ones, it brings us inner pain, brokenness, sadness and grief.

Father in **Ecclesiastes 3:2:** Your word says - *A time to be born, and a time to die; a time to plant, and a time to pluck up that which is planted.* Lord we are aware that the time of death will come so today we are praying that we will be wise enough to be willing to receive eternal life that you offer us before we die.

O Lord, today I pray for the bereaved families. I pray for healing and comfort at this time of sadness. Lord, your word said that it is an appointment to man once to die and after death comes the judgment. O Lord God almighty, only you can give the kind of comfort that the bereaved families need in such a sad time. Only you can dry the tears from their eyes, only you can embrace them to you and heal them. O God, there are times when words cannot explain how the bereaved families feel when their loved ones pass away. Lord, please wrap your loving arms around all bereaved.

Sovereign Lord, I ask you for courage, comfort, and strength. Father, I ask for peace and calmness. I ask for confidence, wisdom and strength. Lord, please let your love surround the bereaved families and heal them from anxiety and depression. Lord, I ask that death will bring the family closer together as they share their sorrows. Lord, help them to appreciate each other in life because death separates families but life can bring unity, love and joy.

O God, I ask that you send all the help that they need, both financial, emotional and physical help. I thank you that your love is able to give eternal life to everyone if they are willing to surrender to you before they die.

According to **John 3:16** you provided help for us before we die: *For God so loved the world that he gave his only begotten Son, that whosoever believeth in him should not perish, but have everlasting life.*

Father, my hope is in you. Help me to give my life to you before I die, because there is no repentance in the grave. O Lord, please help me to repent and turn to you before it is too late. Help me to place values upon my life and live for thee, so that I can receive eternal life, and not to receive your judgments.

O Lord, I ask for your mercies. In the name of Jesus, I pray.

Amen

Prayer for the Children

A Parent's Prayer for Their Unborn Baby

PSALM 127:3

Lo, children are a heritage of the LORD: and the fruit of the womb is his reward.

HOW great is my God, how great is His name. Lord, you are greater than anyone or anything that we can ever think or imagine. According to **Isaiah 64:8*** you are the potter, and we are the clay. Lord, I am aware that the clay cannot tell the potter what vessel to make, but the potter decides what design or what vessel he will make.

Lord, you have the authority over the existence of humanity and over the universe. You are in charge and you are in control.

I give thanks and praise to your wisdom, your power, your knowledge and your authority, you are Lord all by yourself.

Father, according to **Psalm 127:3.** I thank you that you have released a child into my womb as a special gift. I declare that this child will be a real blessing to you, to me and to everyone for your glory.

Lord, I pray for my unborn child and for everyone who is carrying a child. I pray that you will cleanse blood streams from any contaminations that may want to attack unborn children. Lord, I pray that these children will be nourished in their mother's womb to be healthy and strong. I pray for every bone and every organ of these children to function in the way that you have designed them to function.

I pray against any kind of sickness or disease. I pray against any form of complication that may want to attack the children in the womb. In the name of Jesus, I declare wellness, by faith I speak life into the womb. I believe that this child will be born healthy and strong.

Father, before this child is born, I now give them to you for your service, just as Samuel was given to you to serve you and your people. I give this child to you. I declare that this child will be a special child that will listen to your voice and desire to know more about you. Lord, as this child grows, help this child to be in submission to your word and to be a great blessing to your kingdom.

Mighty God, I believe that you are well able and capable to hear and answer my prayers of faith. In the mighty name is Jesus, I pray.

Amen.

*Full Scripture: Isaiah 64:8 [Bible Citations pg 209]

Prayer for the Children - Part 1

EPHESIANS 6:1-3

¹ Children, obey your parents in the Lord: for this is right.
² Honour thy father and mother; which is the first commandment with promise.
³ That it may be well with thee, and thou mayest live long on the earth.

LORD, I just want to thank you for the record concerning children obeying their parents in the Lord. O God, I understand that long life comes to us with the act of obedience. In **Deuteronomy 6:4-9*** you have called upon the parents to teach their children in the way of the Lord so that it will be well with them. Lord, I am aware that the responsibility of the children is rested upon the shoulders of the parents to teach them about life and its true morals.

Lord, I pray that all parents will aim to be good parents. I pray for our children, that they will obey the teachings of your word that all things will be well with them. Father, I ask that the children will follow your lead and your directions in life, so that your love will be demonstrated through them.

Please give the children the wisdom to make the right choices in life, so that they will be able to live a life of godly principles and godly characters.

O Lord God, I ask that you will protect the children from all accidents and dangers. Cover the children and help them to aspire to excellence in all that they do. Lord, let your blessings brings favour into the lives of the children. O Lord, I pray for open doors that will allow the children to identify themselves as the children of God.

Lord, I ask that you will close every door of deception and confusion, and open the doors of opportunities and favours for our children.

O Lord, I ask for a special anointing upon my offspring so that they will place values upon their lives. Lord, please let my children have a spiritual impact on the lives of other children, so that they will come to know you in a real way. These mercies I ask in Jesus' name.

Amen.

Full Scripture: Deuteronomy 6:4-9 [Bible Citations: pg 209]

Prayer for the Children - Part 2

PROVERBS 6:20

My son, keep thy father's commandment, and forsake not the law of thy mother:

WONDERFUL, merciful Father, creator of heaven and earth, it is very necessary for every one of us to know what you require of us in our everyday life. Just as King Solomon was instructed, in **Proverbs 6:20** we also need to take instructions for our moral everyday life values.

Lord, I give thanks to you for the children. Please help all parents to observe your words. Help us to know that you have given us responsibilities towards the children. Father, please help us to obey your words. Help us to teach our children about you, according to **Deuteronomy 6:7**: *And thou shall teach them diligently unto thy children and shall talk of them when thou sittest in thine house, and when thou walkest by the way, and when thou liest down, and when thou risest up.*

Lord God, as we teach our children about you, we pray that they will listen and obey your words. Help them to increase in wisdom, knowledge and understanding so that they can obtain blessings from you and your name will be glorified. Lord, help our children to have a thirst for you, help them to shine and radiate in this dark world.

Holy God, I thank you that you desire that children will grow in spiritual maturity. Help them to be transformed by the renewing of their minds. O Lord, I declare a blessing upon the lives of my children. I declare good health and prosperity upon all children. Father, I pray that our children will be wise enough not to allow bad influences to destroy their lives. Help them to submit to your will and your purpose for their lives. Merciful Father, help me as a parent to set good examples. Help me to build my relationship with my children through prayer.

O Lord, take away every bad spirit, every disobedient spirit, every rebellious spirit from my children, let it not come near them. I command these spirits to go to the pit of hell and remain there. Lord, I pray that you will destroy every plan of the enemies that may want to give bad influence to my children.

Lord, I cover my children under your divine blood. O Lord, I pray for your protection over my children. Lord, give them discernment and discretion, so that they will be able to identify what is right from wrong. O Lord, I pray for my children, I commit them into your care. O Lord, use them for your glory.

Mighty God, I declare your salvation over my children. In the name of Jesus Christ, I pray.

Amen.

Prayer for Peace

Prayer for Peace - Part 1

ISAIAH 26:3

Thou wilt keep him in perfect peace, whose mind is stayed on thee: because ye trusted in thee.

LORD, this morning I declare *Isaiah 26:3**: over my life. Lord, you have promised me that you will keep me in perfect peace, if my mind stays on you, because I put my trust in you.

Lord, I honour you, I worship and I adore you. Lord, I thank you for the special gift of peace; my heart shall not fear or be troubled because you are keeping me safe. O Lord God, many times, I struggle to maintain this wonderful gift of your peace because of fear. Gracious God, I am aware that it is the enemies' plan to rob me of my peace and to bring me into a place of confusion and torment. Lord, you are always assuring me to maintain my peace.

Father, I am aware that the absence of your peace is confusion, frustration, depression and every kind of worry. Lord Jesus, please remind me that you have taken away the curse of sin so that I can become the righteousness of God in Christ Jesus. Lord, you have rooted up confusion from my life, and you have given to me your peace, as a very special gift, to support me and protect me in this wicked and confused world.

O Lord, please help me to know the values and the benefits of your peace. Help me to know the privileges and the blessings of your supernatural peace. Help me to know that one of the reasons that you came to earth was to seal me with your divine peace.

Today Lord, I embrace your peace and I am securing your peace. I am now eating and drinking from the fountain of your peace. Merciful God, I choose to live in your perfect place of your peace all the days of my life. I denounce the spirit of war and confusion, I refuse the spirit of anxiety and frustration; I reject torment and restlessness, for I am resting in you Lord Jesus. I receive courage and comfort in the mighty name of Jesus Christ.

Sovereign God, I thank you for being Lord over my life. I have confidence to receive blessings from your peace because I am now living in you, and you are living in me. Lord, I worship and praise your Holy name.

Amen.

*Full Scripture: Isaiah 26:3 [Bible Citations pg 209]

Prayer for Peace - Part 2

MATTHEW 5:9

Blessed are the peacemakers: for they shall be called the children of God.

O LORD God of peace, I worship and adore your name. I thank you God, that you are my supernatural peace. Mighty God, you are the Prince of Peace.

Lord, I ask that the gift of your peace will be an active force in my life so that I will be able to bring calmness and assurance to those that are disturbed and confused.

I thank you for the wisdom that you have given to me, so that I am able to make a difference wherever I go. Father, help me to keep your peace even in difficult times and to demonstrate your love to others.

I thank you Lord, that you are the maker and originator of peace. Lord, I thank you that your precious peace is living and active in me every day, because you have chosen to anoint me with your perfect peace. Because I trust in you, you have promised to keep me in perfect peace.

Lord, if there is anyone living in a place of fear and confusion, please help them to come to you for help. I thank you O Lord, that you will not turn them away. Eternal God, I ask that your peace will be active in me, as you have full control on this earth to bring peace even into a hopeless situation.

Lord, I ask for your mercies in the name of Jesus.

Amen.

SCRIPTURE VERSES FOR PEACE*

Psalm 119:165*: *Great peace have they which love thy law...*

Psalm 34:14*: *Depart from evil, and do good; seek peace, and pursue it...*

Romans 16 20*: *And God of peace shall bruise Satan under your feet...*

Philippians 4:7*: *And the peace of God which passeth all understanding...*

*Full scriptures: Psalm 119: 165, Psalm 34:14, Romans 16:20 [Bible Citations: pg 209], Philippians 4: 7 [Bible Citations: pg 210]

Prayer for Peace - Part 3

JOHN 14:27

Peace I leave with you, my peace I give unto you: not as the world giveth, give I unto you. Let not your heart be troubled, neither let it be afraid.

MIGHTY God, blessed and holy is your name. I magnify you O Lord, because you are gracious and awesome, you are full of love mercy and compassion.

I am so thankful for the gift of peace. Sovereign Lord, your peace has given me confidence to trust in you regardless of my situation. Your peace has transformed my life so that I can live and feel relaxed with you. Lord, I am confident that your peace is real in my life.

I thank you Lord that you have transformed my life, for where there was war and confusion, you have replaced it with your peace. Where there was torment and fear, you have given me the assurance of your peace. Today I am at peace with you and with man, because you have placed great values upon my life.

Lord, because of your peace, I shall live worshipping and adoring your name. Not by my might, or by my power, but by your Spirit that lives in me. Might God, I shall read your word and live in prayer to build up my relationship with you daily. Because of your peace, I have hope, I have confidence, I have rest, I have joy, and I have strength. Hallelujah.

O Lord, please help me not to be foolish to allow anyone to rob me of this precious peace that you have given unto me. Lord please help me to be wise to treasure this great gift of your peace.

I thank you Lord, for hearing and answering my prayer. I pray in the name of Jesus Christ.

Amen.

*SCRIPTURES VERSES FOR PEACE**

***Psalm 4:8:** I will both lay me down in peace ...*

***2 Thessalonians 3:16:** Now the Lord of peace himself give you peace...*

***Galatians 5:22:** But the fruit of the Spirit is love, joy, peace ...*

*Full scriptures: Psalm 4:8, 2 Thessalonians 3: 16, Galatians 5: 22 [Bible Citations: pg 210]

Prayer for Protection

PSALM 46: 1-4

¹ God is our refuge and strength, a very present help in trouble.
² Therefore will not we fear, though the earth be removed, and though the mountains be carried into the midst of the sea;
³ Though the waters thereof roar and be troubled, though the mountains shake with the swelling thereof Selah.
⁴ There is a river, the streams whereof shall make glad the city of God, the holy place of the tabernacles of the most High.

LORD GOD ALMIGHTY, I look to you, for you are where my help comes from. As I walk with you today, may your divine blessings sustain me and brighten my partway.

Holy Father, I give you thanks for always being by my side in times of trouble, in times of sorrow, and in times of danger. O Lord, you have promised that you will be with me.

Lord, I believe that you are my refuge and my strength. I believe that you are a present help to me when I am in trouble. I believe that your glory surrounds me with the goodness of your love and peace. Lord, my hope is in you and I shall not fear, no matter how the waters of life roar and be troubled. There is a provision; there is a river, there a source of life, to water and to refresh me.

Lord, please help me to walk by faith and not by sight. Help me to believe you even in difficult situations. Even when it seems as if there is no hope, Lord, help me to know that you are always with me and you have already defeated the enemy on my behalf.

Lord, please help me to build up my confidence and assurance in you. Lord, you are well capable to support me, and you will cause me to be victorious. Deliver me from every negative word and action. Please help me to be positive in the way I think and act.

Help me to pray in humility and be obedient to your words. Help me to love others as you command me. Lord, please let the power of your word lead in my life. Praise God, praise God Hallelujah.

Father I thank you for hearing and answering my prayers. In the holy, exalted name of Jesus, I pray.

Amen

Prayer of Assurance in God

PSALM 75:6-7

*⁶ For promotion cometh neither form the east, nor form the west, nor from the south.
⁷ But God is the judge: he putteth down one, and setter up another.*

LORD, it is to you I give the glory. It is to you I give the praise, for you are my hiding place. I bow my knees and worship you O Lord, for you alone are holy, you alone are worthy to be praised. Lord, I thank you for being in partnership with me. I thank you that you are responding to me, directing me according to your will.

Lord Jesus, you are the Christ of my life, you are the Anointed One. Lord, you are the only one that I have confidence in to promote me. I am assured that your word is the signpost to my promotion, not only in this earthly life, but also into eternal life.

Lord, I thank you for this blessed assurance, and I believe that my strength will rise when I wait upon you. I understand that I cannot face everyday challenges without your help. Father, help me to have all the confidence and the assurance that you are with me at all times.

Lord, I did nothing good to deserve your presence or your loving kindness. Nevertheless, you O Lord, you have granted me favours of every kind. I thank you for your blessings. I thank you that you are daily supplying me with benefits.

Lord, I thank you for always assuring me that you are with me, and that you are protecting me and you are bringing down every stronghold of the enemies on my behalf. Please help me to be alert. Lord, please help me to be watchful and to keep my focus, that no weapon that is formed against me shall prosper, and every tongue that speaks against me is already condemned in judgment, because you are with me.

Lord, please help me to have enough confidence to know that you have seated me in heavenly places, and you have given me the authority to have dominion over my enemies or over anything or anyone that may want to stop my spiritual growth. I shall not be defeated, because you O Lord are by my side and I shall triumph. Hallelujah to Jesus!

I thank you Lord for this blessed assurance. In the name of Jesus, I pray.

Amen.

Prayer for a Change of Heart

PSALM 51:10

Create in me a clean heart O God; and renew a right spirit within me.

O LORD my God, how excellent is your name in all the earth. I worship you, dear Lord, I bow my knees before you and I called you Holy, I called you worthy, I called you Lord, I call you King of Kings and Lord of Lords. Father you alone are worthy to be praised, from the rising of the sun unto it's going down. Lord, you are a great God.

Father, just like David prayed, and asked you to create in him a clean heart, so I pray for a clean heart. Lord God, only you can make that change in me. Lord, only you can transform me.

Mighty God please grant me the willingness to allow you to make that change in me.

The heart that I was born with was contaminated by sin, it was wicked and evil. Mighty God, I seek a clean heart, a heart that will obey your word, a heart that is humble and committed.

Lord, according to **Hebrews 10:16*** you have promised that you would write your words in my heart and in my mind. Father I embrace this glorious promise.

Today I open my heart's door to you. I open my mind for your words to enter in and for you to do a transition. O Lord, it is my desire to submit to your will, so that your love can draw me closer to you. Father, **Philippians 4:7** says: *And the peace of God, which passeth all* *understanding, shall keep your hearts and minds through Christ Jesus.* Mighty God, help me to get rid of the old carnal and sinful nature so that your peace can lead me and guide my heart and mind.

Lord, help me to get rid of the old ways of thinking. Lord, help me to get rid of the old heart and mind that wanted to hold me captive. Allow your holy words to wash me and make me clean. Lord Jesus, please let your Holy Spirit transform my mind to a new way of thinking so that I will be able to do your will.

Gracious God, I am yearning for a heart like yours, a heart of love, mercy and compassion. A humble heart, a heart of willingness and commitment. Lord please give me a heart to help those that are in need. O merciful God, please help me always to speak words that will give healing and not words to hurt or wound anyone. Lord, help me to give words of comfort that will strengthen the sad and the broken. Father, if my heart is bad and wicked, I will not be able to do your will. O my God, I cry out unto you to help me to be honest with whatever I do, in Jesus name.

Lord, I thank you for hearing and answering my prayer of faith. In the name of Jesus, I pray.

Amen.

*Full scripture: Hebrews 10:16 [Bible Citations: pg 210]

Prayer of Thanksgiving for a New Heart

MATTHEW 11:29

Take my yoke upon you, and learn of me; for I am meek (gentle) and lowly (humble) in heart, and ye shall find rest unto your souls.

LORD, I thank you for a new heart; I thank you that I am learning to be obedient to do what you have designed me to do for your glory. I thank you that my heart is now in fellowship with you.

Lord, I thank you that you have stripped away every stubbornness, bitterness, strife and self-will, so that I can be your vessel.

I thank you for taking away my weakness and replacing it with your strength.

You took away discouragement and replaced it with encouragement.

You took away fears and doubts and replaced them with confidence and trust.

You took away ignorance and replaced it with knowledge and understanding.

You have taken away anxiety and replaced it with calmness and serenity.

You have taken away poverty and given me richness.

You have taken away sadness and given me joy.

You have taken away confusion and given me peace.

My heart is fixed; my mind is stable to absorb the love of God.

My heart is renewed like the eagle, and I am soaring with the almighty God.

My heart takes pleasure in the Lord and I delight to have more of His wisdom.

I am so grateful that God had a plan for my life even before the foundation of the world to give me a new heart. I am now lavishing my life in the abiding peace of God. I position my life to keep my eyes on the word of God because it is my signpost to eternal life. I am praying my way out of spiritual poverty and anything that may want to hold me captive. I have wrapped myself with the mantle of prayer, praise and worship to the God of heaven.

God's plan for my life is perfect; I receive favour as I wait on the Lord. In the mighty name of Jesus Christ, I pray.

Amen.

Prayer for Good Health

Prayer for Good Health - Part 1

JEREMIAH 17:14

Heal me, O LORD, and I shall be healed; save me,
and I shall be saved: for thou art my praise.

O Lord, God of all grace, God of might and power, I worship you, I adore you, for you are a loving God. You are the God who looked beyond my faults and saw my needs. Lord, it is you who has opened up the doors of healing and given everyone an opportunity to receive healing by faith.

Lord, your words say in **Matthew 7:7**: *Ask, and it shall be given you; seek, and ye shall find; knock, and it shall be opened unto you.* So today Lord Jesus, I declare healing for every kind of sickness and disease that may want to attack my body.

Lord, in **Isaiah 53:5** you told us that: *But he was wounded for our transgressions, he was bruised for our iniquities, the chastisement of our peace was upon him; and with his stripes we are healed.*

Mighty God, I really appreciate what you have done. Lord, you have carried my shame and grief, my pains and our sorrows to the cross; you have suffered so that I can receive healing, emotionally, physically and mentally.

Lord, thank you for the price that you have paid for me to receive salvation. According to **Isaiah 53:5:** Your body was pierced and beaten for my peace and healing. God, I cannot pay you for what you did for me, so today I want to say thank you, Lord Jesus.

Today I speak the blood of Jesus over my body. I speak the blood of Jesus over everyone and everything that is attached to me. I declare good health in my body in the mighty name of Jesus. I refuse to allow any kind of sickness or disease to live in my body. I command my body to function in good health by the blood of Jesus.

O Lord, it is all about what you have done for me. You have redeemed me and you called me your own. Lord, you put your Holy Spirit into my body so that I can be your temple where you dwell. Lord, I have received your words of healing today; I command my body to line up with the word of God and live free from every kind of infirmity.

I thank you for the power of prayer, Lord. By my faith, I use your powerful word to perform healing in my body.

Lord, I give you thanks with a grateful heart; I thank you for your mighty power and healing for good health. In the name of Jesus, I pray.

Amen.

Prayer for Good Health - Part 2

3 JOHN 1:2

Beloved, I wish above all things that thou mayest prosper and be in good health, even as thy soul prospereth.

FATHER, I give you praise, because you cared for me and you have placed great values upon my life. Lord, you are the one that has designed my body, but there are many different types of sicknesses and diseases, that cause distress, pains, discomfort and all types of un-pleasantness.

Lord, I thank you that I can still have a merry heart because of my hope of salvation.

According to **Proverbs 17:22,** you remind us that: *A merry (cheerful) heart doeth good like a medicine: but a broken (crushed) spirit drieth the bones.* Father, help me to receive your word for my medicine to perform your healing power in my body.

Your words declared, in **Psalm 139:14:** *I will praise thee, for I am fearfully and wonderfully made.* Lord, please remind me to declare the power of your word in faith over my body to keep me in a healthy lifestyle. I refuse to allow sickness and disease to overpower my body. Lord, I shut the door of sickness and disease over my life and my family.

Lord, I declare your word over my life according to **Psalm 107: 20*.** You have sent your word to heal me, and to deliver me from destructions, so right now O Lord; I have received your word. I have recognised you to be my healer:

I speak against anxiety and depression.

I speak against Alzheimer and dementia diseases.

I speak against heart diseases and lung diseases.

I speak against cancer, lupus and sickle cell diseases.

I speak against kidney malfunction and abnormality, and every other kind of disease.

According to **Psalm 147:3***, you have promised to heal the broken-hearted and to bind up their wounds. Today I declare that the door of sickness is closed and no sickness shall manipulate or control my body.

Lord, I thank you for good health. I pray in the name of Jesus Christ.

Amen.

*Full scripture: Psalm 107:20, Psalm 147:3 [Bible Citations: pg 210]

Prayer for Healthcare

PSALM 121:1-2

¹ I will lift up mine eyes unto the hills, from whence cometh my help.
² My help cometh from the LORD, which made heaven and earth.

O LORD, my God Almighty, how excellent is your name in all the earth. The heavens and the earth bow down before you and reverence your holy name. Eternal God, you alone are God all by yourself. You alone are my maker, you alone are the life giver. Mighty God, there is none like you, and there is none to compare with you.

This morning I am presenting the healthcare workers before you. They are people who you are using to help those who are suffering health problems. I ask that you will strengthen them and keep them in good health. Lord, please help them to be strong to do whatsoever they are assigned to do. Lord, I ask that you will help them to depend always to you for help. Merciful God, please help the doctors, the nurses, and the ambulance services. Lord, please help all the carers, the cooks and the cleaners, the receptionists and porters, and all the support workers. I pray for everyone who works tirelessly to help in the care system.

Please give them the right ideas, and the understanding to know what to do when they are dealing with dangerous and difficult cases. Lord, help them to trust you and depend on you to show them what to do, for the benefit of themselves and for the people who are in their care. Merciful God, I pray that you will give them wisdom, knowledge and understanding so that the lives that they are responsible for will receive good benefits, and they will be healed in the mighty name of Jesus.

Lord, today I declare a blessing upon the lives of all care workers. Lord, I appreciate their services and dedication. I want to say thanks to them for all the help that they give to the public. Many times, they put their lives at risk; many times, they put their lives in danger to help others. Father, I pray that you will encourage and strengthen them, help them to know that their labour of love will not be in vain. Lord, the Covid-19 pandemic has taken many lives to the grave without a hope in you.

O Lord, today I am praying that all people will all come to know you in a real way before they die. Please help us all to know that you are Lord over our lives. As I study the work manuals, I will also study the Bible and build my relationship with you, so that I can receive salvation.

Lord, I thank you for hearing and answering my prayer of faith. In the name of Jesus, I pray.

Amen.

Prayer for Victory Over Depression

Prayer for Victory Over Depression

PSALM 46:1

God is our refuge and strength, a very present help in trouble.

LORD, I thank you that you are my hiding place. You are my high tower in the time of trouble. I thank you Lord, that you have not forsaken me. I lift up your name in high regards, for you are a Holy God. Just like David experienced you as his refuge and strength and a present help in trouble. So I declare you as my help.

Lord, I am aware that many different types of health problems can cause depression. Today I refuse to live in depression. I refuse to allow my life to waste away by depression or by any plans of the enemy that may want to depress me and to hold me captive. I am now taking charge over my mind, and I am allowing my mind to take courage in your word. I speak to my mind to focus on you alone. I turn my mind away from the wrong ways of thinking. I will resist fear, discouragement, self-pity, anxiety and depression.

I refuse to allow my mind to hold me captive. I bind up every spirit of confusion, depression and every contrary action of the devil. I command my mind to leave the place of doubts and fear, and to line up with the word of God. In the name of Jesus, I uproot my mind from the place of depression and command it to live in the place of peace and harmony with the word of God.

Merciful Father, you have promised that you will keep me in perfect peace if my mind stays focused on you. I now position my life and recondition my mind to live by your word. Lord, according to *2 Timothy 1:7** you have reminded me that you did not give me a spirit of fear, but you had given me the spirit of power and of love and of a calm (sound) mind.

Today I embrace the spirit of your powerful word. I am willing to live with a fresh mental and spiritual attitude. I refuse to allow fear to dominate my life. I am willing to renew my mind in your spirit and hold on to the power of your love to maintain a sound mind. O Lord God, I thank you for releasing me from depression and frustration. I rise up and take a stand that nothing shall hold me captive. I am set free from the evil works of the devil by the blood of Jesus. I am set free from the barrier of fear in the mighty name of Jesus Christ.

Romans 8:28* says that all things are working together for my good, because I love you, and I am called according to your purpose. Lord, I believe that all things are working together for my good because I love you. Lord, you have called me for your purpose. I am willing to carry out your assignment in the power of your strength.

I declare victory in the name of Jesus Christ. Lord, I honour and I glorify your name for you alone are worthy to be praised.

Amen.

*Full scripture: 2 Timothy 1:7, Romans 8:28 [Bible Citations: pg 210]

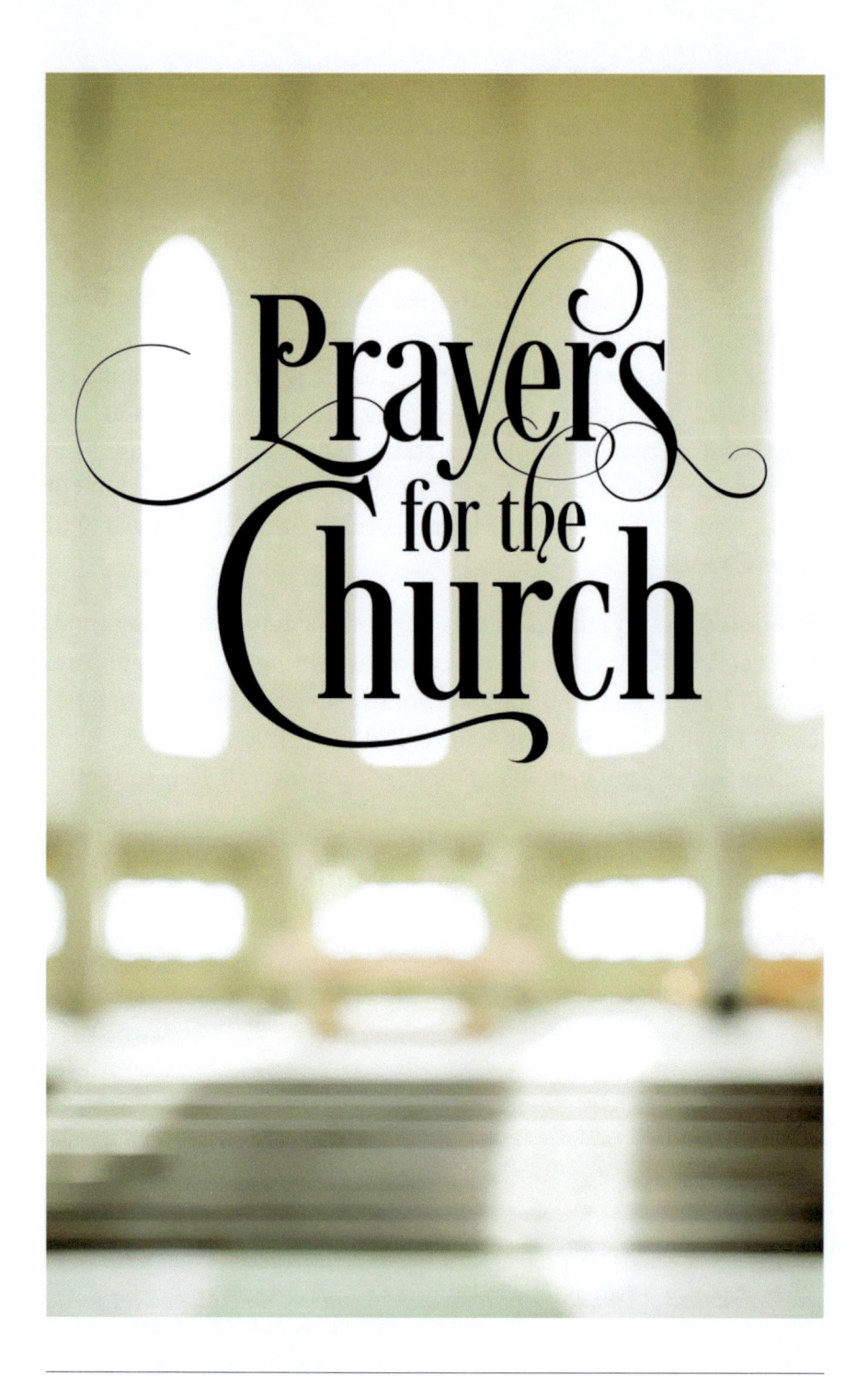

Prayers for the Church

Prayer for the Church - Part 1

THE church is not a religion, or an organisation; it is not the walls of a building. The church is not a money-making business. The church belongs to the Lord Jesus Christ, the God of creation. The church is called the body of Christ, and we often gather for fellowship, for prayer, praise, worship and thanksgiving to the God of heaven. Jesus said in **Matthew 21:13:** *It is written, My house shall be called a house of prayer; but ye have made it a den of thieves.*

The church is a spiritual body of people who have answered the call of God. God has designed His church to be a spiritual and educational centre, to educate people about their creator. We can only join the church by being born into the church by receiving the Holy Spirit.

The Holy Spirit appointed people to preach and to teach people from the Holy Scriptures, about their creator for the saving of souls. All spiritual leaders should be led by the anointing power of the Holy Spirit of God, and not to preach or teach by their own knowledge, desires, options or personal views.

Let us pray

Wonderful, merciful Father, precious redeemer and King, we give thanks to you for the spiritual body (called the church). Lord, we thank you that you are able to fill the church with your wisdom, knowledge and spiritual understanding. Help us to demonstrate tender mercies and compassion towards others.

Lord, empower the church with your love and humility; help us to be patient with others. Lord, help us to be with one accord and in unity with each other. Help us to forgive others so that your name will be glorified. Father may your bond of perfectness and your peace rule our hearts.

Help us to allow your Holy Spirit to enlighten us, to empower us and to unveil your words to us.

Help us to plant honesty, to reap trust.

Help us the plant goodness, to reap a good harvest.

Help us to plant humility, to reap greatness.

Help us to plant consideration, to reap the right attitude.

Help us the plant perseverance, to reap satisfaction.

Help us to plant hard work, to reap success.

Help us to plant forgiveness, to reap reconciliation.

Help us to plant faith and reap spiritual growth.

Help us to be careful of what we are planting now, because it will determine what we reap later.

O Lord, help us to be humble as we walk in your calling. Merciful God, we thank you for hearing and answering our prayers of faith. In the name of Jesus Christ, we pray.

Amen.

Prayer for the Church - Part 2

MATTHEW 16:18

Upon this rock, I will build my church, and the gates of hell shall not prevail against it (or conquer it).

ALMIGHTY God, creator of heaven and earth, to your name be praise, to your name I give all the glory and all the honour. Lord, your name is above every other name. At your name, every knee shall bow, and every tongue shall confess that you are Lord.

Eternal God, thank you for designing your church to be the carrier of your word. Lord, your word is able to transform me and keep me from the bad influences of this wicked world.

Father, I understand that you are building your church on the truth and the revelation about you. If the church is not about you, there is no hope or life for the believers.

Lord, I believe that the church is a body of people who have answered to your call. A people who are willing to obey and follow all your instructions Just like the holy prophets and the apostles carried out your instructions. Recorded throughout the Holy Scriptures.

Father, your word declared in **Acts 2:38**: *Then Peter said unto them, Repent, and be baptised every one of you in the name of Jesus for the remission of sins and ye shall receive the gift of the Holy Ghost (Spirit).* Lord God, your word was so effective that about three thousand souls received salvation. God. I thank you that they used the formula that you gave them.

Father, please let your church be humble and willing to speak your word with power and authority. Let your word be the pillar of our faith. Father, in **Matthew 24:35** your word says: *Heaven and earth shall pass away but my word shall not pass away.*

Lord, you honour your word; that even if the heaven and earth pass away, your **WORD** will last forever. Eternal God, please fill your church with the Spirit of your word. Mighty God, help your church to be obedient to your word and make us ready for your return.

Gracious God, let your Holy Spirit bring hope to your people, that we will find peace in you. Lord let your church be in fellowship with you at all times. Let your church preach and teach the gospel, which is the good news about you.

Sovereign Lord, eternal God, you alone are worthy. Lord, please help us to submit and surrender, to serve others in love, with the right attitude and in humility.

Father, please strengthen the body of Christ. O Lord Jesus, I thank you for hearing and answering our prayers. Lord, we ask it all in the name of Jesus.

Amen.

Prayer for the Church - Part 3

EPHESIANS 4:4-6

⁴ There is one body and one Spirit, even as ye are called in one hope of your calling.
⁵ One LORD, one faith, one baptism.
⁶ One God and Father of all, who is above all, and through all, and in you all.

MIGHTY God, I thank you that you have called your people into one body, for you are one Lord, and you have called us into one faith, and one baptism. This is the way of unity, because you are the ONE Father of us all.

Lord, please give us wisdom, knowledge and understanding to live in obedience of your word. Help the church to fast and pray against every spirit of opposition, every spirit of deception and oppression. Lord, let your love flow in your church. Mighty God, I declare blessing upon your church. I declare the anointing that was on David be poured out upon your church, for there are many spirits of Goliath that may want to threaten your people.

Transferred the faith that was in Abraham upon your church to journey with you, regardless of how rocky and tiresome the road may be. Lord, let the courage that was in Elijah be in your church, to call fire down from heaven so that all people will know that you are the true and living God.

Mighty God, let the church receive favour from you just as you granted Peter, James and John at the Mount of Transfiguration.

They saw something greater and more powerful about you. Let the anointing power that was upon Peter be upon your church to speak your word with boldness, just as he preached on the day of Pentecost. One message caused about three thousand souls to receive salvation according to **Acts 2:41***. Father, your word is powerful and active, to enter into the hearts of man, and to change lives.

Mighty God, let the anointing that was on Apostle John be upon the church. He was willing to suffer for your name, even when he was held captive on the island of Patmos. Lord, you have unveiled deeper revelations about the future to him.

Lord, let your church be willing and bold to preach your word even in the face of opposition, just like Apostle Paul. Take away the spirit of fear and replace it with confidence. Lord, please take away the spirit of sleep and give your church alertness, please help us not to be distracted but to keep our focus on you.

Holy God, please take away the spirit of self-will, and allow your Holy Spirit to lead your church into victory. In the mighty name of Jesus Christ, I pray.

Amen.

*Full scripture: Acts 2:41 [Bible Citations: pg 211]

Prayer for Discernment

EPHESIANS 1:17

That the God of our LORD Jesus Christ, the Father of glory may give you the spirit of wisdom and revelation in the knowledge of him.

FATHER, in the name of Jesus, I give thanks to you for the spirit of discernment, the spirit of enlightenment, the spirit of revelation, the spirit that is able to unveil the mystery of your words to me in this dark world. Lord just like Apostle Paul prayed for the Ephesians brethren so that you will give them the spirit of wisdom and revelation to know you, so I pray that you will grant to me discernment.

Lord, I ask that you will help me to discern what is wrong from what is right. Lord, please open the eyes of my Understanding and enlightened me grant me your Spirit of wisdom, knowledge and revelation, so that I can know more of you. Lord, please give me the ability to have wise judgment. Father, help me to listen to your voice, so that I can discern what is your will and purpose for my life for your glory.

Lord, help me to examine my motives concerning the things that I do or say. Gracious God, I ask that you will help me to make wise decisions. Give me insight and foresight that I will be able to look into the future, so that I will be able to distinguish between the wise and the unwise. In *Acts 5:3, 9-10**, Peter was able to discern the deception of Ananias and his wife Sapphira. In *Acts 16:18**, Paul was able to discern the spiritual source of a girl's fortune-telling ability. Lord, please empower me with discretion so that I will be able to speak wisely. Please give me the spirit of discernment, so that I will be able to judge well, and I will be able to identify the true spirit from the false spirit.

Father, please let your Holy Spirit take active force in my life so that I will not be foolish, but I will be wise. I will not be blind to the things that I should see. Please help me not to be absent when I should be present. Lord, please put a watch upon my tongue, so that I will know when to speak, and what to say.

Lord, help me to observe your word and be obedient. O Lord, help me not to allow anyone to manipulate or confuse my mind against what your word commands me to do for your glory. Father, let your spirit of discernment lead me and guide me. Help me to walk the path of truth that you have mapped out for me.

Lord, I thank you for transferring me out of the kingdom of darkness to the kingdom of light. I thank you that you have a plan and purpose for my life.

Most Holy God, even though I sometimes do not understand what you want me to do for you, I pray that you will help me to know your will. Help me to follow in your footsteps and into your divine plan for my life.

Holy God, thank you for hearing and answering my prayer of faith. In the name of Jesus, I pray.

Amen.

*Full scripture: Acts 5:3, 9-10. Acts 16:18 [Bible Citations: pg 211]

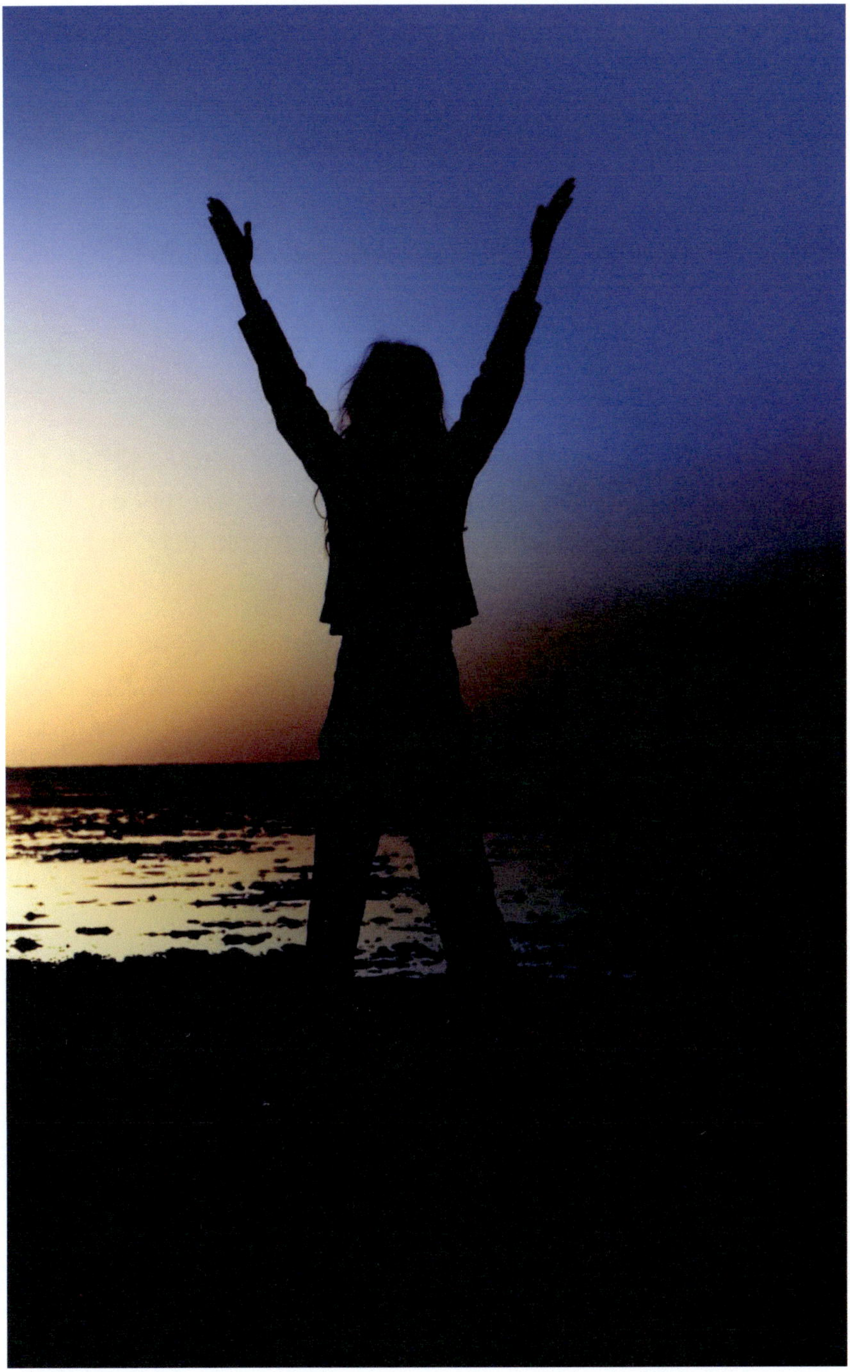

Prayer for the Police Force

PSALM 32:8

I will instruct thee and teach thee in the way which thou shall go: I will guide thee with mine eyes.

MERCIFUL, wonderful saviour, precious redeemer and King, this morning I rise from my bed to say thanks you for another day. Lord, this is the day that you made for me to give thanks unto you. Lord, without you my life would be meaningless.

Mighty God, just like King David had confidence in you to ask you to teach him and to guide him in the right way, so I ask for the police force. God, I ask that you will teach them, and guide them in the right direction.

Lord, according to *1 Timothy 2:1-2** you have asked us to pray for those who are in authority. Lord, I come to you in obedience of your word. I am presenting the police force before you. Lord, these are people who have been appointed to seek out the welfare of vulnerable people. Help them always to remember that they are the law enforcers who are supposed to bring security and justice to society, as they depend on you for wisdom, knowledge and understanding.

This morning I am praying for the protection and safety of the police force. Sometimes they put their lives in danger to help the vulnerable. Lord, I pray that you will stand by the police force at all times. Give them the awareness to identify danger, for their own safety and the safety of the public.

Merciful Father, I pray that the police will always be aware that all human beings are important to you and they must be treated with respect and good care. Please help the police not to use their authority to abuse or brutalise the public and destroy lives, to satisfy their own emotions, because we are all human with feelings. Guide them so that everyone may live a quiet and peaceable life, in all godliness and honesty.

Father, I pray the police force will submit to your rule so that they will recognise you and know that you have the greater rule over them. Most of all I pray for their salvation, that they will come to know you in a real way. My God, help the police force to seek after you. Let compassion lead and guide them into a close relationship with you so that their souls will be saved.

Lord, I thank you for hearing and answering my prayer. In the name of Jesus, I pray.

Amen.

*Full scripture: 1 Timothy 2: 1-2 [Bible Citations: pg 211]

Prayer for Those Who Are in Prison

PSALM 28:1

Unto thee will I cry, O LORD my rock; be not silent to me: lest, if thou be silent to me, I become like them that go down in the pit.

FATHER, in the name of Jesus, I give thanks to you for grace. I thank you that we do not have to slay an animal as a sacrifice for our sins. Lord, you have asked us to repent, to turn away from sins and you will forgive us and cleans us from all unrighteousness.

Father, just like David cried unto you and you helped him, so I cry to you on behalf of those who are in prison. Lord I pray that every prisoner will start crying out to you for help. Lord, I believe that you will not be silent to them, but you will help them and deliver them.

Father, I understand that laws are in place, to bring justice and clarity, to address issues or problems that may confront us in life. Father, I pray for those that may be guilty of a crime or may not be guilty, but somehow they find themselves behind bars. Lord, I ask for your grace to change them. Help them to repent and receive you as their Lord, for you will pardon them.

Merciful Father, I ask that you will be the councillor, and advocate for those who are held captive. Lord, I know that sin is the force that causes people to do the things that are wrong and evil, but Lord, I ask you for mercy and compassion on their behalf.

Merciful Father, I ask that you will give the prisoners a thirst for you during times of distress and weakness. Lord, as they reflect on the things that they have done wrong that causes them to be in prison, please give them a heart that is turned towards you. Lord, please help them to confess their sins and repent (apologise) for the evil that they have done. O God, please give them healing and grace as their hearts submit to you and the law. Lord, I know that prison is no barrier for you to work on the hearts of humans. I ask that you will show compassion for their repented heart, change their lives from the evil forces of darkness, and transfer them into the kingdom of light. Please help them to turn away from doing evil.

Mighty God, I ask that you will forgive their sins and be their advocate. I ask that you will transform their minds and use them to bear witness of you in the spirit of truth, so that they will tell others about your saving power. Break their chains, O God, and use them for your glory. I ask for your mercies, in Jesus name. Amen.

Lord, I pray for those who are not guilty of a crime. I ask that you will show compassion and mercy upon them. Lord, I pray that you will release them from bondage. Father, many families may be mourning for the false accusations on the lives of their loved ones. O God please let the truth be revealed. Father, please be their advocate and stand with the innocent in the court room and speak on their behalf, be their solicitor, O Lord, be their judge, and help them to be released and returned home to their families. Lord, let not the innocent be punished any longer.

Thank you Lord Jesus for hearing our prayers as you bring deliverance to the innocent. In the name of Jesus, I pray.

Amen.

Prayer for those who are Taking Exams

116 | IT IS TIME TO PRAY

Prayer for Those Who Are Taking Exams

1 CORINTHIANS 2:9

But as it is written, eye hath not seen, nor ear heard, neither have entered into the heart of man, the things which God hath prepared for them that love him.

O GIVE thanks unto the Lord for He is good, for His mercy endures forever. Lord, I honour you and I glorify you for your goodness. I thank you for your loving care. Lord our eyes and our understanding is limited to see and to understand the things that you have prepared for all those who love you. Today I pray that everyone will start loving you, and will receive favour from you to have a bright future.

Merciful God, I ask for your help for everyone who is preparing to take their exams. Lord, I ask that you will sit with them in the exam room. Lord, please help them to remember the things that they have studied, so that they can give the correct answers.

Holy God, our future is in your hands. Your word says that eye has not seen, ear has not heard. Neither has it entered into the heart of man, the things that you have prepared for those who love you.

In *Deuteronomy 31: 6** you encouraged Joshua to be strong and to be of good courage. Lord, I ask that you will give courage to those who are taking exams. Please take away fear. Take away distractions and confusion. Lord, please give them stability of mind to keep their focus, so that they will have the confidence to do their work well. O Lord, help them to have wisdom, knowledge and understanding. Father, I ask that you remind them that you are able to help them to pass their exams with excellence.

Most of all Lord, I pray that they will acknowledge you in everything that they do, and that they will surrender their lives to you. Lord, I ask that you will open the understanding of everyone to focus on your word for prosperity, as they look forward to a brighter future.

Lord God, please help them to have a bright future in life, and they will trust in you. Lord Jesus, I believe that you have heard and answered this prayer concerning all those who are taking exams. I ask your mercy, in the name of Jesus, we pray.

Amen.

*Full scripture: Deuteronomy 31:6 [Bible Citations: pg 211]

Prayer for the Homeless

Prayer for the Homeless

PSALM 41:1

Blessed is the man that considereth the poor: the LORD will deliver him in time of trouble.

O LORD, I give thanks unto you for your loving kindness. I thank you Lord, that you are our provider. Father we are sustained and kept by you.

Gracious God, I thank you for providing a home where I can lay my head, when I am tired and weary. Lord, I am conscious of many people that do not have such privilege or such an opportunity.

Lord, today in humility, I am praying for all those who are homeless. I am praying for help, because it is a very sad situation to be homeless. It is sad to know that people are sleeping outside.

O Lord, I pray for help for humanity. Humans are not designed to live outside in the cold. Many times my heart is broken, and I feel helpless when I am not able to help them more than to pray for them, and to give them some food. Father, I pray that their situation will be turned around and they will get some help. I pray for shelter, I pray for comfort and warmth. I pray for food and clothing. Mighty God open doors for the homeless.

Lord, there are times when I reflect on you, when you were on earth. There may have been times when you also faced the same situation of homelessness. According to **Matthew 8:19-20,** a man asked to follow you, and these words were your answer: **Verse 20**: *And Jesus* *saith unto him, the foxes have holes, and the birds of the air have nests; but the Son of man hath not where to lay his head.*

Father, I thank you that you became poor and for me, so that I may become rich. You became homeless so that I can rest in you. Holy Father, your word says that a man's life does not consist of the abundance of things that he possesses *(Luke 12:15)*. I understand that, naked we came into the world, and naked we shall return. I am not asking for riches, fame or fortune but I am asking for moral help for life, not only in the natural but also in the spiritual.

O most high God, I ask that the homeless will understand that you have made provision for them to live eternally. Lord, please help humans to seek ways to share with others, so that we can make a difference in their lives. Help us to show love for each other because we are our brother's keeper. Help us to understand that when we show love we are demonstrating your characteristics. Loving others is a perfect way to lead people to you.

Holy Father, I ask for your divine help, mercy and compassion on behalf of the homeless, so that they will have a safe place where they can live and rest and meditate on you. Merciful God, please save the homeless, dear Lord. Please give them a change of lifestyle not only in the natural but also in the spiritual, so that they can testify about your goodness and your name will be glorified.

Hear my prayer O God. I ask for your mercy, in Jesus name.

Amen.

Prayers for Marriages

Prayer for Marriages

GENESIS 2:24

Therefore shall a man leave his father and mother, and shall cleave unto (unite with) his wife: and they shall be one flesh.

FATHER, I give thanks to you for all marriages. I thank you for humanity and the way you provide for us. Lord, there is nothing missing that you have forgotten to provide for us in this life and in the life to come.

Eternal God, your original plan at the beginning of creation was for marriages to work following your instructions.

Holy God, today I call upon you on behalf of marriages. In *1 Corinthians 7:3** we learn that the husbands should fulfil their marital duties to their wives and likewise the wives to their husbands. Lord, help every husband and wife to come to the full understanding of what you expect of them. If they follow your instructions, they will enjoy a peaceful and successful marriage.

Lord, I thank you for the instructions that come from you concerning a successful marriage. Please help each husband and wife to live by the law of love. Marriage is not a comedy show. It is not a life of abuse and unhappiness. It is not a life of disrespect, selfishness and confusion, but it is a life of LOVE. The absence of love will open the door for confusion to enter. This is an opportunity for the enemy to bring separation.

Ephesians 5:25: you have called upon the husbands- *Husbands love your wives even as Christ also loved the church, and gave himself for it.*

Mighty God, I ask that you will help both the husband and his wife to understand each other. Help them to be willing to love and respect each other. Lord, help them to value each other. Help them to care for each other. O mighty God, I pray that husband and his wife will share their life together in love. They will pray together so that their relationship with you, and each other, will become stronger and stronger.

Hebrews 13:4: *Marriage is honourable in all, and the bed undefiled (kept pure): but whoremongers and adulterers God will judge.*

Lord, I understand that marriages may sometimes face some challenges. As two people come together to become ONE, there will be many adjustments and many changes they will need to do for them to become ONE. Lord please give them an understanding heart. Help them to know that their marriage is honourable and their coming together is pleasing to you. Lord help them not to withhold themselves from each other but to respectfully enjoying each other.

Please help all couples to be humble and wise to put their trust in you. I pray they will have the right attitude towards each other. Lord, please show your love so that it will be accomplished in their lives, and wherever they go, your name will be glorified.

In the mighty name of Jesus Christ, I pray.

Amen.

*Full scripture: 1 Corinthians 7: 3 [Bible Citations: pg 212]

Prayer for Husband & Wife - Part 1

GENESIS 2:18

It is not good that the man should be alone; I will make him a help meet for him.

Sovereign Lord, it is a good day to praise your name, regardless of our circumstances, regardless of our situation. Lord you deserve all the praise all the glory and all the honour.

Mighty God there is always a need to pray and I believe that when we pray you will answer. Today I am praying for husband and wife.

Father, in **Genesis 2:18** your word said: *It is not good that the man should be alone; I will make him a help meet for him.*

Lord, for this reason you provide a woman for the man to be his wife, so that they can have a loving and caring relationship with you and with each other. Lord, you have designed them to live into a loving relationship.

I thank you for the goodness of your grace. I thank you O Lord, that when you designed men and women, you desired for them to live their lives into a unique way. You wanted them to enjoy each other and to have a happy lifestyle. Lord, you have made man in your own image to have fellowship and relationship with you and with each other. You have designed the man and his wife to produce life on the earth. O Lord God, I am thankful.

From the beginning, the enemy was not in agreement with your word or your plans concerning the man and his wife, so he came in the midst of them to interrupt your plans, to interfere with your plans. Yes Lord, the enemy came to stop man from having fellowship with you by the act of disobedience. O God, I thank you that you are so rich in mercy, that you have provided grace. You have opened new doors by the demonstration of your love, so that man can have a new relationship with you and with his wife.

In *Ephesians 5:22-23:* you call on wives: *[22] Wives submit yourselves unto your own husbands, as unto the Lord. [23] For the husband is the head of the wife, even as Christ is the head of the Church: and he is the saviour of the body.*

Father, please help every husband and their wives to observe and obey your words, and to live by them, just as you have commanded them. Help the husband to consider the way that you love the church, and he will match it with the way he loves his wife.

Lord, please help husbands to know that you have designed them to be the head of their house. Lord, just as you are the head of the church, help them to know that they supposed to be a source of support and protection around their family.

Father, I ask for your mercies. In the name of Jesus.

Amen.

Prayer for Husband & Wife - Part 2

ZACHARIAH 4:6

Not by might, nor by power, but by my Spirit saith the LORD of host.

O LORD God, as I examine what is happening around me, it seems as if many husbands are still in the Garden of Eden. Many are still distracted by the lies and deceptions of the serpent, that old dragon Satan. Lord God today, I speak **Zachariah 4:6** over every husband and their wives. Lord, it is not by their might or by their power but it is by your Spirit that they will overcome the attack of the evil one.

I pray that the husbands will be observant and constantly use the power of your words to protect their wives from the words of the serpent. O Lord, please open the eyes of the husbands that they may see. Open their ears O God, that they will hear you speaking to them to use your word against the attack of the enemy.

Lord, it is time for Adam to speak your word with power and authority. Lord, please shake up the husbands, and help them to put on the armour of righteousness, so that they can fight the spiritual warfare. Help them to live right and to be honest, committed to prayer and fasting.

Father, just as you allowed Samuel to anoint David, I ask that you will anoint the husbands so that every yoke of the enemy that comes to bring distractions will be broken. Every deceiving and contrary spirit will be silent. Lord, please help the husbands to have the right spiritual attitude. Help them to be aware of their responsibilities, and to lead their wives and family in the right spiritual direction in prayer and submission for your glory.

Help both husbands and wives to look out for the strategies of the enemy. Help them to be alert, and watchful and to be protective of each other, not to be abusive and selfish towards each other just because they are frustrated with life. O my God, I cry out to you for marital relationships.

Lord, please unveil to every husband and wife your wisdom, knowledge and understanding. Help them to understand that you are depending on them to be of a good example for your glory. Lord, please work a miracle upon them and transform their minds. Take out the spirit of selfishness and bitterness and replace it with your love.

Take out the spirit of un-forgiveness and replace it with a heart of forgiveness, love, mercy and compassion. Lord, restore hope to husbands and their wives. Break down every separating wall so that they can have a healthy and a happy family life. O Lord God, I give you thanks for hearing and answering my prayer of faith.

Lord, I ask for your mercies, in the name of Jesus Christ.

Amen

Prayer for Husband & Wife - Part 3

PSALM 1:1-2

¹ Blessed is the man that walketh not in the counsel of the ungodly, nor standeth in the way of sinners, nor sitteth in the seat of the scornful. ² But his delight is in the law of the Lord; and in his law doeth he meditate day and night.

O LORD God, of all grace might, power and authority. I give thanks to you for husbands and wives. I pray that husbands will be wise men. Lord plant them by the rivers of water that they will bring forth in its season. Fruits that are desirable. Fruits that bring forth spiritual life.

Lord help the men to have strong a backbone to stand up for your words to direct their lives.

Lord, please help husband to be loving and kind, merciful and compassionate. Lord help them to use the right attitude toward their wives and family. Help husbands not to see themselves as weaklings but strong in faith. Help them not to depend on themselves, but to depend on you. Lord, help them to understand that you have given them a key to open doors of opportunities in every way.

Lord, please help husbands to know the right ways to use the keys of blessings to have a prosperous and progressive family life. Lord Jesus, please help the husbands to place values on their lives, to seek after godly principles and godly characters, so that they will be a good example to single men. Holy God, help then to think positively and act responsibly. Help them to live a well-balanced life so that they can be progressive and successful husbands.

O Lord, please help husbands to be praying men. Merciful Father, I present husbands and wives to you today, help them to think positively about each other and help them to put you first in everything, for you are depending on them to be good examples. Save the husbands and wives. Deliver them from the plans of the enemies. Break every chain, barrier and every stronghold of the enemy. For the enemies 'plan is to defeat them and to bring them to an open shame.

In **Ephesians 5:22-33*** you gave instructions to the wives, how to submit to their own husbands. Lord, many wives are summiting to their husband and doing all that you ask. Many times, husbands or wives are so abusive, selfish, disrespectful to their spouse, and family. Many times either wives or husbands have to leave the matrimonial home to seek shelter for help. Lord, this type of lifestyle was not your original plan. Merciful Father, please console broken relationships and heal them emotionally. Mighty God, your word said according to **Mark 3:25** *a house that is divided against itself cannot stand*. Father, I speak unity in marriages, bring healing and victory.

I thank you for all relationships that are bonded by love and working for your glory.

Thank you for hearing and answering my prayers of faith, on behalf of husbands and wives. In the mighty name of Jesus, I pray.

Amen.

*Full scripture: Ephesians 5:22-33 [Bible Citations pg 212]

Prayer for Husband & Wife - Part 4

PSALM 1:3

And he shall be like a tree planted by the rivers of water that bringeth forth fruit in its season; his leaf shall not wither; and whatsoever he doeth shall prosper.

O LORD how excellent is your name in all the earth. Your name is above every other name. Your name came to give us hope. I thank you for all your love. Thank you for all your mercies and compassion towards us.

Father, I come to you on behalf of husband and wives. Holy Father, you have designed women to be the mothers for children. It is your plan for humanity to come into the world through a man and a woman. Lord according to **Psalm 1:3** help humanity to rest up on your promise. I ask that we will be like a tree planted by the rivers of water, we will bring forth fruits in its season and whatsoever we do will prosper. Lord please help all husband and wives to look to you, to be fruitful not only in the natural but also in the spiritual.

Lord God almighty, your plan for life, is a glorious and a blessed plan for your glory Lord Jesus. I am aware that many wives and husbands are so sad and broken because their marriage is not working satisfactorily.

Holy Father, many homes are broken and divided, because where there should be peace and harmony, the doors are open to the spirit of confusion. The spirit of deception has broken and destroyed many relationships, and this causes many children to suffer both emotionally and physically.

O Lord God Almighty, I pray for the wives, for many times the burden of the home is upon the shoulders of the wives, to carry the heavy load of the children without the support of their husband. Merciful Father, I pray that you will show kindness to the wives. Please speak into the hearts of their husbands to help their wives with their offspring.

O Lord, society is getting so wicked because the home should be a place of a good foundation for children. Your original plan was not for wives to take the leading role in the home or in the church. Such responsibility was given to the husband. Lord, I pray that men will take up their position and their responsibility to be the men that you have designed them to be. Let the wives be in reverence to their husbands, working together on their relationship just as your word says. Father, it is not a pleasant feeling when marital relationships are broken, because it brings so much inner pain, and sadness for families.

Mighty God, I ask you to intervene and help families who are suffering abuse. Lord, please let your love flow through husbands and wives that their relationships can be a place of safety for the children. O Lord, I run to you for help, for only you can help in such a time as this.

Lord, you are my security; I will continue to pray for the restoration of marital relationships. In the name of Jesus Christ, I pray.

Amen.

Thanksgiving for Husband & Wife Praying Together

PSALM 118:19-20

¹⁹ Open to me the gates of righteousness: I will go into them, and I will praise the LORD:
²⁰ This gate of the LORD unto which the righteous shall enter.

O LORD, God of all grace, we give thanks to you for our marriage. We thank you for all marriages that are working. We pray for unity for those marriages that are not working.

Lord, We thank you for **Psalm 118:19-20** you have open to us the gates of righteousness and as we entered, we are committed to having a loving and lasting relationship, just as you have commanded us in your word.

Holy God, your love will continue to sustain and support us as we continue to keep the unity of the spirit, in the bond of peace. We are willing to follow the laws of **LOVE**, and we are certain to have a healthy marital relationship.

Lord, we lock the doors of selfishness and disrespect that will want to come to cause disruption to our relationship. According to **Mark 3:25,** Lord your word said: *And if a house is divided against itself, that house cannot stand.*

As husband and wife, we will pray together with our children, and we close every door against the enemies. We put you, God, in the middle of our relationship and nothing shall uproot our marriage from your mighty love Lord Jesus. Lord, today, we declare your continual love and peace over our marriage.

As a husband - I will continue to love and respect my wife. She is a **Proverbs 31:10-31*** woman, a virtuous woman. She is wise, she is honest and a vibrant woman of God. My wife loves God and is committed to prayer. She loves and cares for me. My wife is always seeking ways to make me feel special. I love my wife, and I thank God for her. Today I speak supernatural blessings over my wife, and over our marriage in the mighty name of Jesus. Amen.

As a wife, I love, respect and care for my husband. He is a loving, caring and faithful man of God. I love to read the word of God with my husband and discuss the word. As a wife, I am conscious that my husband is the head of the house, even as Christ is the head of the church. My husband and I always take a stand to maintain and secure the peace of God in our home. I feel secure with my husband because I am confident that he will protect me. My husband is always seeking ways to make me feel special. As a wife, I am willing to spend quality time with my husband; we talk, laugh and pray with each other. Today I speak blessings in abundance over my husband, and over our marriage in the mighty name of Jesus. Hallelujah.

Lord, we thank you for unity and honesty in our marriage. We can discuss matters in honesty and in a reasonable way. We seek to understand the feelings of each other. Lord, it is by the power of your word we live to make our marriage a happy foundation together for our family.

Father, we thank you for the standards and principles of a blessed marriage. Today we declare supernatural blessings over our marriage. In the name of Jesus, we pray.

Amen

*Full scripture: Proverbs 31: 10-31 [Bible Citations: pg 212 - 213]

Prayer for My Home & Family

1 CHRONICLES 16:34

O give thanks unto the LORD; for he is good; for his mercy endureth forever.

Lord, I rise from my bed this morning to sing praises unto you. I glorify your name I worship and bow down before you O Lord for you are great. I thank you for your protection and salvation for my family.

I give thanks to you that you have blessed my family and myself with all spiritual blessings in our home. You are a good God to us. O Lord, I really thank you for your enduring mercy.

Lord, I thank you that your blood is able to cover my home and my family. Father, you have enlightened my family to know that you are the God who provides for us. Lord, I welcome the presence of your power that enters into my home each morning. Mighty God, your presence has brought your peace, your healing and your joy into my home. Every morning there is a cool wind of your grace entering my home.

O Lord my God, I declare **Psalm 57:7** over our lives: *My heart is fixed, O God my heart is fixed: I will sing and give praise.*

Lord, by your grace, we fix our heart on you alone, for you are our dependency. Merciful God, you have made my home to be a safe place for my family and myself to live. Whoever enters our front door shall always enter into a place of peace and tranquillity.

Lord, I thank you that your Holy Spirit brings wisdom, knowledge and understanding into my home, so that we can praise you at all times. Because of your Holy Spirit, we are assured that no plague shall come near our dwelling, and no sickness or disease shall invade our home.

Lord, today I declare peace, perfect peace in my home. I denounce every spirit of falsehood and deception from my home. No confusing spirit shall enter my front door. I take authority by your Holy Spirit to release the blessings of God in and around my home.

God, you have blessed my bread and my water, and I shall have enough food in my home to give to those who are in need. My home is a place of prayer and praise to you Lord Jesus Christ. Mighty God, you are the head of my home. My home is filled with your love and my family and I, are resting in your loving arms. Lord, I am so grateful that your blood is in my heart and on the doorpost of my house for our protection. Hallelujah to Jesus.

Thank you for the protection of your blood. Your loving kindness is rich towards my family and me. In the exalted name of Jesus Christ, I pray.

Amen.

Prayer Against Spiritual Warfare - Part 1

PSALM 121:1-2

¹ I will lift up mine eyes unto the hills, from whence cometh my help. ² My help cometh from the LORD, which made heaven and earth.

Praise the Lord, Praise the Lord. God I magnify you Holy name, for you are great and greatly to be praise.

LORD, today I lift up my eyes to you, for all of my help comes from you. Father, I am aware that there is always spiritual and physical war going on in this world, darkness is fighting against Light. Just as David said, he will always seek help from you. Lord, I come in agreement to seek help from you, for you are the light of the world and you are a gracious God.

Lord, according to *Isaiah 54:17**, your word said, no weapon that is formed against me shall prosper; and every tongue that rises up against me, in judgment is condemned. For this is the heritage of the servant of the Lord, because my righteousness is in the Lord. Father in the name of Jesus, by faith I declare these powerful words over my life, and I am using them to destroy every attack of the enemy.

I rise to take authority to condemn every weapon and every tongue that may rise up against my family or me because we are your servants and you have established us in your righteousness.

Lord, because of your divine grace, your blood has protected my family and me from the traps of the evil one. Lord, your word said in **2 Corinthians 10:4:** *For the weapons of our warfare are not carnal, but mighty through God to the pulling down of strongholds.* This morning, I pull down every stronghold of the enemy, with prayer and fasting in the mighty name of Jesus.

Mighty God, I thank you for giving me authority over every force of darkness, over every lying and contrary spirit, over every confusing and tormenting spirit. I command them to depart from my dwelling place. I command them to leave right now and go back to the pit of hell and remain there.

Lord, I receive the power of your anointing that you have released in my life, to protect me from evil. I speak **Psalm 23:4*** with confidence. Even when I am walking through the valley of the shadow of death, I will fear no evil, for you, O Lord, are with me. I speak to every separating wall that the enemy sets against my family and me; I break them down, and crush them right now. In the Mighty name of Jesus.

I declare that we are safe from the plans of the enemy. Lord, I praise your name for the power of your Holy Spirit. Hallelujah to Jesus.

Amen.

*Full scripture: Isaiah 54:17, Psalm 23:4 [Bible Citations: pg 213]

Prayer Against Spiritual Warfare - Part 2

PSALM 25:1-2

Unto thee, O LORD, do I lift up my soul. 2 O My God, I trust in thee: let me not be ashamed, let not my enemies triumph over me.

ETERNAL God, Mighty God, Sovereign God. I exalt your glorious name. Lord you have given me much more than the naturalness of life. Lord you have given me your Holy Spirit to look out for me, and to defend me, so that my enemies cannot triumph over me. Hallelujah praise God.

Lord, your Holy Spirit is helping me to overcome the tricks and plans of the evil one. Lord, you have made me to be able to discern the plans of the enemies, and you have helped me to defeat them and take control by using the power of your word, in the mighty name of Jesus Christ.

Lord God, in *1 John 4:4* your word said: *greater is he that is in me, than he that is in the world*. Lord, I declare the power of your anointing to bind up all contaminated wells of evil. I come in agreement with the sword of your word to destroy all demonic forces in the name of Jesus.

Mighty God, eternal God, your Holy Spirit is greater and more powerful than every spirit that is in this world. You are able to take action against every force of the spirit of darkness. Lord, please protect anyone who is suffering the attack of evil spirits. Let your holy angels stand with swords drawn to protect your people.

Father, according to **Ephesians 6:10-17***, I stand in faith with your protective shield around me. I am armed with the breastplate of righteousness, and my feet are walking in the right direction. Lord, I am equipped with the preparation of the gospel of peace.

I take the shield of faith, and I quench every fiery arrow of the wicked. Father, I am covered with the helmet of salvation, and I use the sword of the spirit, which is the word of God, to overpower the evil forces of darkness. Hallelujah, praise God.

Mighty God, according to **Ephesians 2:14*** you have broken down the middle walls of partition, and you have given me free access to your throne room. I am privileged to make my request known unto you. Lord, your Holy Spirit has given me new visions, new power and new anointing, to command all powers of darkness to submit to you. Father, you have signed a new covenant with me, so that I can have fellowship and a relationship with you.

Merciful Father, you have given me authority to speak your word over every situation. Today I speak against every spirit of confusion, sickness and disease that may want to enter my body, my family or my dwelling place. I command them to dry up and die instantly.

O Lord God Almighty, I thank you for deliverance from the hands of the enemy. Praise God, I am now living in victory. Hallelujah, praise God. Thank you Lord, for hearing and answering my prayer of faith. In the Holy name of Jesus Christ, I pray.

Amen.

*Full scriptures: Ephesians 6:10-17
 Ephesians 2:14 [Bible Citations: pg 214]

Prayer Against Demonic Attack - Part 1

PSALM 91:14

Because he have set his love upon me, therefore will I deliver him, I will set him on high, because he hath known my name.

HOLY God of all grace, God of wisdom, God of Knowledge, God of all understanding. I give you thanks for your Lordship, for there is none greater or more powerful than you. Lord, I declare **Psalm 91:14** over my life, Lord God, I have set my love upon you; I have confidence in the promise of your word to deliver me, because I know the power that is in your name.

I thank you for dispatching angels to watch over me. I am convinced that my personal strength will sometimes fail me, but your Holy Spirit is strong and powerful enough to shield me at all times. Praise God Almighty.

Lord, according to **2 Timothy 1:7** your word says: *For God hath not given us the spirit of fear; but of power, and of love, and of a sound mind.* I speak to my mind to come in alignment with the word of God right now. I shall overcome every spirit that is not of God.

In the name of Jesus, I come against the spirit of fear. God, you didn't give fear to me, and I don't need it. Fear is a strategy that the enemy uses to captivate people's minds, and to bring them into captivity. Lord, I am allowing my mind to absorb and obey your word to bring me into the place of peace and confidence in you. Satan shall not have dominion over my family or me. We shall not be held captive by fear. Lord, In **Isaiah 41:10*** your word reminds me that I should not be afraid, or be dismayed (distressed), for you are my God. Lord, you have promised to strengthen and help me.

In the name of Jesus, I come against Satan's plans and strategies. I bind up old bad habits and attitudes, confusions and all ungodly thoughts. I bind up fear and emotional pains. Lord, I take authority over the spirit of un-forgiveness. I take authority over every contrary and tormenting spirit. I come up against every spirit of depression and anxiety that may want to attack my mind and to put sickness and disease upon my body. With the power of your Holy Spirit, I pull down Satan's kingdom, for it shall not be progressive in my life.

Lord, I root up old ideas and bad desires. I pull down and break every strong hold of the evil forces of Satan, and I send them back to the pit of hell.

Lord, according to **Zechariah 4:6:** *Not by might, nor by power, but by my Spirit saith the LORD of hosts.* Father, I am holding onto the fragrance of your word, I shall not be discouraged or distracted. I cannot do your work by my might nor by my power, but by your Spirit. Yes Lord Jesus, please let your Holy Spirit take active force in my life to accomplish your work through me.

Father, I have confidence that I can accomplish the work that you gave me to do. I am letting go of my own opinions, my might and my power. Lord, I hold on to your Holy Spirit to empower me. Father, your Holy Spirit is powerful enough to defeat, to destroy, to break down and to crush every attack of the enemies.

Lord, I give you thanks for deliverance. I am now free from every demonic attack of the enemy. Hallelujah to Jesus, praise God.

Amen.

*Full scripture: Isaiah 41: 10 [Bible Citations: pg 214]

Prayer Against Demonic Attack - Part 2

ISAIAH 43:11

I, even I, am the LORD; and beside me there is no saviour.

HOLY Father, King of my life, God of the universe, how excellent is your name in all the earth.

Lord, I thank you for the power of your word. Father, please help me to always activate my faith, to speak your word over my life. Mighty God, I believe that your word is in your blood, and your blood is in your name. Lord, there is no God beside you.

Today I declare that by the power of God, I am delivered from every trap and every attack of the enemies because of your name. I have confidence that your word is able to protect me even when I am sleeping. Lord, I believe that your word is a living organism, it is growing, it is increasing, your word is active, to produce fruits in my life for your glory. Hallelujah.

Holy God, you have given me the authority to speak your word over my mind to be stable in your word. According to **Matthew 17:20*** your word said that if I have faith as small as a grain of mustard seed, I can speak to this mountain, and it shall move out of its place, and nothing shall be impossible for me. Lord, whatever the mountains are, that may want to block me or distract me, I speak against them, and I command them to move out of my way, in the name of Jesus.

By the power of God, I command every trap and every enslaving yoke to be broken right now. I cut and clear every rope. I dismantle every chain that is set up to bind me into captivity. I set myself free right now, in the mighty name of Jesus Christ. Lord, I thank you that you have given me the authority to use the sword of your word, to disconnect my life from every demonic attack of the enemies. I root up and destroy every seed that is sown by the enemies against me and my family that they shall not grow. I bundle them up and I cast them into the furnace of hell fire. Lord, I thank you that it is over now. Hallelujah.

The enemy shall not defeat me, because the blood of Jesus Christ has given me wisdom to be victorious and prosperous. I shall bear spiritual fruits, and not only leaves, because God has planted me by the rivers of water. His Holy Spirit is watering me daily to produce fruits for his glory. Hallelujah.

Lord, I thank you that your super-natural power has destroyed the works of Satan on my behalf, and I am now living in confidence. According to **1 John 4:4*** Lord your word said: *greater is he that is in me, than he that is in the world.*

Holy Father, sovereign God, eternal God, I thank you that your Holy Spirit is in me, and you are greater than the spirit that is in the world. There is no power that is greater than your power.

Lord, I receive protection and security from you at all times. Thank you Lord Jesus. Hallelujah. Amen and Amen. Praise God.

Amen.

*Full scripture: Matthew 17:20
1 John 4:4 [Bible Citations: pg 214]

Prayer for God's Help

PSALM 27:14

Wait on the LORD: be of good courage, and he shall strengthen thine heart: wait, I say, on the LORD.

LORD I rise out of my sleep this morning to give you all the honour and all the glory that is due unto your name. Lord, it is a blessing for me to embrace **Psalm 27:14.** I determine to wait on you and to be of good courage while I am waiting on you.

Father, I take courage to wait upon you, because you are my strong tower, you are my hiding place. Lord, every morning I open my treasure box, and I am empowered with new strength, I receive healing, and encouragement. Lord, as I open my treasure box, I receive eternal life through the power of your Holy Spirit.

Lord, please help me to patiently wait upon you. Hallelujah.

Lord I believe that:

Your power will pilot me and direct me in the right direction.

Your strength will sustain and keep me.

Your wisdom will enlighten me, and guide me to make the best decisions.

Your eyes will look ahead for me, to see the things that I am unable to see.

Your ears will listen for me, and your Spirit will alert me.

Your hands will protect me and carry me when the road gets rough and tiresome.

Your love will embrace and empower me, to complete your work.

Lord, you have planted me into your vineyard, and I shall not be uprooted by anyone. I shall not be moved out of my place, because I am sustained and kept by you the Lord God Almighty. Lord, you are my rock and my high tower. I will not spend time trying to work out any problems, for you have already worked it out for me. Your eyes are watching out for me, so that I can relax and trust in your timing. I will rely on your promises, and wait for your blessings.

Holy Father, I thank you that I can depend on you, and I can trust you. O Lord, you will never let me down. You are helping me to live the way you want me to live. You are helping me to love the way you want me to love.

Sovereign God, you have heard and answered my prayers. Father, you are always helping me. Lord, even when I am sleeping and I am unconscious, you are doing the night shift for me. Hallelujah.

Lord I am willing to give the way you want me to give, and love the way you want me to love.

I am committed to please you O Lord. I thank you for all of your help towards me, and towards everyone. In the mighty name of Jesus Christ, I pray.

Amen.

Prayer for a Friend Who is Sick

A good friend is like a treasure box with great values. They allow people to feel comfortable and secure, by being kind and confidential. A friend seeks to be generous and is always willing to help when there is a need, without the expectation of getting something back in return. A friend seeks to give wise council, encouragement and words of hope. Praise God.

Let us pray

Jeremiah 17:7: *Blessed is the man that trusted in the LORD, and whose hope the LORD is.*

O LORD my God, how excellent is your name in all the earth. The heavens and the earth bow down in respect to honour you and to show forth your glory.

Lord, you know the importance of a good friend. When your friend Lazarus died, you were emotionally broken, and you cried. This was a demonstration of love.

Lord, I thank you for choosing a good friend for me. At this time my friend is sick, and is feeling sad and broken. Lord, I am asking you to grant favour. By faith I pray that my friend's mind comes out of depression and anxiety. I pray deliverance from past hurts and pains. Lord, please release your anointing oil upon my friend, perform a transition to give hope and comfort. Lord, please work a miracle and bring healing not only physically, but emotionally and spiritually as well.

I come in agreement with your word, according to *Jeremiah 30:17*: *For I will restore health unto thee, and I will heal thee, of thy wounds, saith the LORD.* I speak life over my friend. I speak healing in the mighty name of Jesus Christ. I believe that your divine word is taking active force to restore healing to my friend right now. I declare that both mind and body are healed, bones and marrow are healed, blood vessels are healed, brain cells, memory cells, and every organ in the body are healed in the mighty name of Jesus Christ.

Lord, I have experienced you to be a healer to me. I am confident that whatsoever I ask according to your will is available for the sick. Lord, with much confidence, I believe that my friend has faith in you, and we now come in agreement with this prayer. I believe that your healing power is activate, and healing is taking place right now, in the mighty exalted name of Jesus Christ.

Lord, I am also asking for healing for everyone who is sick and is hurting. Mighty God, we are all living into a sad and hurting world, a fearful and a confused world. Father, we are depending on you to help us in everything.

Lord, I thank you for hearing my prayer of faith, in the mighty name of Jesus.

Amen.

Today I am Receiving My Miracle

PSALM 103:1-5

¹ Bless the LORD, O my soul: and all that is within me, bless his holy name.
² Bless the LORD, O my soul, and forget not all his benefits:
³ Who forgiveth all thine iniquities; who healeth all Thy diseases; ⁴ Who redeemeth Thy life from destruction; who crowneth thee with loving kindness and tender mercies;
⁵ Who satisfieth Thy mouth with good things; so that Thy youth is renewed like the eagles.

LORD, today I command my mind to worship you in the beauty of holiness. I come in agreement with your word to perform miracles in my life. I thank you for forgiving my sins. You have saved my life from destructions. You have crowned me with your loving kindness and tender mercies. You have satisfied my mouth with good things, so that I am renewed like the eagle's mouth.

Isaiah 59:19 says: *When the enemy shall come in like a flood, the Spirit of the LORD shall lift up a standard against him.* It is a day of miracles. It is a new day when God is knocking on my door, to continue new page in my life. The Spirit of God is at work, lifting up a standard against the enemy. I thank you that your miracle key is unlocking every door that shut against me. Lord, you are opening new doors of healing and blessings for me. I declare that this new day is bringing me new strength, new courage, new wisdom, new knowledge and new understanding. Hallelujah, praise God.

Sovereign God, mighty God, by faith I am receiving my miracle right now in the mighty name of Jesus Christ. I have confidence that you are working in my favour right now mighty God. Lord, I believe that every yoke and chain is broken from my life right now. I believe that every fear, every anxiety and depression is removed. Every negative way of thinking that wants to hold me captive, I destroy it and I denounce it right now by the blood of Jesus Christ. No weapon of the enemy shall be used against me. Lord, I find shelter in you and I am safe in the mighty name of Jesus.

Lord God, you have never run out of power to perform miracles. I rest assured in you Lord Jesus. I am relying on you to perform your word in my life. Gracious God, I believe that you have shed your blood on Calvary for my safety, healing and deliverance.

O Lord God Almighty, today I have received my miracle and a new life in you. Lord, I thank you for the miraculous change that is taking place in my life right now. I shall never be the same from this moment on. Lord, I glorify your name. I worship you dear Lord, for this great change in my life. Praise God. Hallelujah.

In the holy, exalted name of Jesus Christ, I pray.

Amen

There is a Higher Power Than Our Natural Power

1 CORINTHIANS 2:14

But the natural man receiveth not the things of the Spirit of God: for they are foolishness unto him: neither can he know them, because they are spiritually discerned.

Lord, you are my security, you are my hiding place, you are my high and strong tower. I am safe in you alone because you have reassured me with an overflowing of your blessings.

As we read the word of God, we will understand that without the Holy Spirit of God inside of us, we are only natural. We need to be born again of the Spirit of God to experience a new spiritual birth. We all need to receive Jesus Christ and he will direct us of how we can receive a new life in him. This is call repentance or the turning away from sin, as record in **Acts 2:1-47***.

Acts 2:38 says: Then Peter said unto them, Repent, and be baptized every one of you in the name of Jesus Christ for the remission of sins, and ye shall receive the gift of the Holy Ghost. This message of repentance caused about three thousand souls to receive salvation.

According to **John 3:1-7***, Jesus and Nicodemus had a conversation concerning the new birth. This conversation opened the doors of our understanding concerning the two different types of nature, and the two different types of birth. The Holy Spirit will help us to live a righteous life so that we can receive eternal life in Jesus Christ.

1 Corinthians 15:50 *says: Now this I say, brethren, that flesh and blood cannot inherit the kingdom of God; neither doth corruption inherit in-corruption.* This means that we all need to have a changed life, and this happens when we are born again to receive eternal life.

Romans 8:9* says that if we do not have the Spirit of God, we are none of His. This means that the Holy Spirit will transform us from the natural to the spiritual, so we can have a personal relationship with God and eternal life with God, who is the true Spirit.

Let us pray

LORD, I believe that I need your Holy Spirit to have eternal life in you. I surrender to you Holy God. I repent of my sins right now. Please help me to make this change. I will humble myself to seek you daily.

I need your Holy Spirit inside of me to protect and guide me, to support me, and empower me to live a life of holiness for your glory. In the name of Jesus name, I pray.

Amen.

*Full scriptures: Acts 2: 1-47 [Bible Citations: pg 215 - 217]
John 3: 1-7 [Bible Citations: pg 217 - 218]
Romans 8: 9 [Bible Citations: pg 218]

Praise & Worship to the God of Heaven

I understand that everyone can praise God. We praise God for what he has done for us. However, we **worship** God for who He is.

Psalm 150:6 says, *Let everything that hath breath praise the LORD. Praise ye the LORD.* It is a great privilege and opportunity, to honour, to praise the true Lord God of heaven.

In *Psalm 148:1-14,* David called upon the hosts of heaven, the sun and moon, the shining stars, the highest heavens and the deepest waters to praise the Lord. Because He is the creator of them all.

In *John 4:23-24.* [23] Jesus said: *But the hour cometh, and now is when the true worshipers shall worship the Father in spirit and in truth: for the Father seeketh such to worship him.* [24] *God is a Spirit: and they that worship him must worship him in spirit and in truth.*

The Lord God is still seeking true worshippers that will worship Him in spirit and in truth. I understand that a true worshipper is a person that is fully empowered with the Holy Spirit of God. One that is loving, merciful, committed, sincerely living the word of God, and is willing to do the will of God. A person that is kind and compassionate, one that is faithfully preaching and teaching the true gospel about Jesus Christ. One that is honest, helpful and is willing to serve people, whether they are rich or poor. A true worshipper is not oppressive, arrogant or partial, but allows the wisdom of God to lead them at all times.

Let us pray

LORD, I am reflecting on your characteristics, and I am trying to measure up my life with your word. I want to know if I am a true worshipper or not. I am seeking to produce the qualities of a true worshipper for you. Lord, you have chosen and called me. You have set me apart to be a true worshipper of you.

I praise and worship your holy exalted name for there is no weakness or limitations in you. You are the all-wise God, the almighty God, the everlasting Father, the King of Kings and the Lord of Lords. Father, there is no one like you, there was no god before you, and there will be no god coming after you. Father, there is no one greater than you, there is no one more powerful than you, and no one to be compared with you. Lord God almighty, you are God all by yourself. You do not need to seek council from anyone, you alone are worthy to be praised and worshipped.

Mighty God, I give you all the honour, all the glory and all the praise. I exalt you O God, for you are worthy to be praised from the rising of the sun and at all times of the day and night.

I wrap myself into your arms and relax my mind to praise and worship you with a true heart. Hallelujah to Jesus Christ our Lord. Praise God.

Amen.

The Love of God in Action

Jeremiah 31:3: *The LORD hath appeared of old unto me, saying, Yea, I have loved thee with an everlasting love: therefore with loving kindness have I drawn thee.*

John 3:16: *For God so love the world, that he gave his only begotten Son, that whosoever believeth in him should not perish but have everlasting life.*

John 13:34: *A new commandment I give unto you, that ye love one another; as I have loved you, that ye also love one another.*

Matthew 22:37-39: [37] *Jesus said unto him, Thou shalt love the Lord thy God with all thy heart, and with all thy soul, and with all thy mind.* [38] *This is the first and great commandment.* [39] *And the second is like unto it, Thou shalt love thy neighbour as thy self.*

1 John 5:3: *For this is the love of God, that we keep his commandments: and his commandments are not grievous.*

John 15:13: *Greater love hath no man than this, that a man lay down his life for his friends.*

1 John 4:7-8: [7] *Beloved, let us love one another: for love is of God; and every one that loveth is born of God and knoweth God.* [8] *He that loveth not knoweth not God; for God is love.*

1 John 4:20-21: [20] *If a man say, I love God, and hateth his brother, he is a liar: for he that loveth not his brother whom he hath seen, how can he love God whom he hath not seen?* ²¹ *And this commandment have we from him, that he who loveth God, love his brother also.*

Romans 5:8: *But God commendeth his love toward us, in that, while we were yet sinners, Christ died for us.*

Let us pray

O LORD God Almighty, you have proven your love to man before the beginning of creation until now. I thank you for all your loving kindness; I thank you for considering me when I had no hope. Lord, please help me to follow your examples of your love. Help me to receive revelations of who you are to me, so I can love the way you want me to love, and I will give the way you want me to give, so that I can make a difference in this world.

Father, your commandments of love are powerful and true, and they are important to me. Lord God. Merciful God, your love has made a difference to me and I am grateful. Sovereign Lord, let your name be glorified, let your name be exalted at all times because of your divine love. In the name of Jesus, I pray.

Amen.

Words of Hope - Part 1

The word 'hope' means: to have a desire for a particular thing to happen. It is a feeling of trust, to cherish a desire with anticipation, for something to happen or to be fulfilled. (Source: Oxford Dictionary).

Isaiah 41:10

Fear thou not; for I am with thee: be not dismayed;
for I am thy God: I will strengthen thee; yea, I will help thee; yea, I will uphold thee with the right hand of my righteousness.

Just like God spoke to Israel through the prophet Isaiah, in **Isaiah 41:10** so he is speaking to us today. God is still saying "FEAR NOT FOR I AM WITH THEE".

NO matter how stormy or how dark the times of life may be, never let it bring you down to a place of hopelessness. God said fear not, for He is with us. God has promised to help us and to hold us up. Be encouraged and strengthened with what God says to us. Because God is with us, He will take care of us. God is our helper and provider; he will always give us his divine blessings. Hallelujah.

Look in the mirror, and speak the following words with confidence, for personal encouragement:

I will always trust in the name of Jesus Christ, the Lord God Almighty.

I will never give up on myself, because God is with me.

*I will **never*** stop believing in myself.

*I will **never*** doubt myself, because God has given me confidence.

*I will **never*** become over-anxious for anything.

*I will **never*** stop praising and worshipping God.

*I will **always*** pray and build my relationship with God.

*I will **always*** believe good things about myself.

*I will **always*** live and hope for a brighter future.

*I will **always*** remember that I am valuable in the eyes of God.

*I will **always*** walk by faith and not by sight.

*I will **always*** seek to live in peace at all times.

*I will **always*** give to those who are in need.

*I will **always*** love and care for my family and all people.

*I will **be quick*** to forgive those who may hurt me.

*I will **allow*** the Holy Spirit of God to lead me.

*I **love God*** and I love his people.

*I **refuse*** to be jealous or envious of anyone.

*I **refuse*** to render evil for evil.

God's protection is over me, and I shall not be afraid.

Praise God.

Words of Hope - Part 2

My hope is in the almighty God. I am building on the foundation of faith. I receive strength, wisdom, knowledge and understanding to stay in fellowship with God.

I shall live in God's protection at all times. I have total confidence that God is watching over my family and me. I believe that God is sustaining and keeping us for His glory.

According to **Psalm 34:7** it says: *The angel of the LORD encampeth round about them that fear him, and delivereth them.* I declare that the angels of the Lord are camping around my dwelling place continuously. They are on assignment to protect my family from every evil force of darkness.

I shall not be dismayed for God is with me, and He is sustaining and taking care of my family and me every day. I am assisted by the hand of almighty God and I am strengthened and increasing my faith in him. The blessings of God make me rich and fill my heart with joy. God has listened to every prayer that I pray, and He is changing situations in my life for His glory and for my benefit.

God has separated me and set me apart from worry, anxiety, and every depressive situation for His service. Praise God. I shall cross every Red Sea, every Jordon River and every Jericho wall that stands in my way. I declare them to come down by the power of the Almighty God. I will use the power of prayer, and the power of praise and worship to defeat everything that may come against my health.

I receive revelation from God to understand the spirit and power of his word. I look beyond the naturalness of life and see the spiritual works of God operating in my life. Praise God.

Let us pray

Father, in the name of Jesus, I thank you that your divine presence is with my family and me. We shall not be discouraged, for you are our God. Our hope is in your promises to strengthen and to protect us.

Father, we have confidence to find hope in your word to accomplish your will. Thank you for hearing and answering our prayer of faith, in Jesus name we pray.

Amen.

Protection in Jesus Christ

I have confidence that the Almighty God of Abraham, Isaac and Jacob, the God of heaven and earth is protecting me from all different types of challenge and danger at all times.

According to **Joshua 1:9*:** God commanded Joshua to be strong, and to be of good courage. He should not be afraid or be dismayed for He will be with him. Just as He was with Joshua, let us embrace the same words and believe that God is with us.

God's promises are sure if we only believe. I am confident that God is protecting and sustaining us everywhere we go. God has proven His faithfulness to Joshua, and to all His holy prophets and apostles, and He will do the same for us.

I believe that God is my shield and my hiding place. God is daily loading me with benefits, and He is always giving me sufficient grace to protect and shelter me from every storm of life. God has caused me to be a conqueror. I will always use the word of God and He will always honour His words, to defeat the plans and the tricks of the enemy on my behalf.

Let us pray

Lord, I will not be afraid because you are my God and I put my trust in your word. I shall not live in fear or doubt because you choose to live in me and I am available to be your temple. No spirits of disturbance shall come near my dwelling place because you are with me. I declare that my mind shall never feel intimidated by any evil spirits of this world. I am encouraged by you almighty God, that you are capable to guide every step that I take.

Sovereign Lord, I refuse to walk in any direction that you are not leading me. God you has promised me that you will never leave me or forsake me. I am embracing your words, to lead me and to guide me, all the days of my life for only in you I am safe.

I refuse to allow the weakness of my flesh to rob me of your blessings for my life. I refuse to miss the inheritance that you have promised me.

Lord, I am dwelling in the secret place where you are hiding me. Your wings are covering me like a blanket. When sorrow surrounds me like a flood, and the stormy wind of life blows to defeat me, I am protected and safe in you. I shall not be shaken, weak or discouraged because I am anchored in your love.

According to **Philippians 4:13**, *I can do all things through Christ, which strengthens me.* Lord, I am standing in the power of your word. I am standing in faith, to allow your word to be my driving wheel, to lead me in the right direction. O Lord God almighty, I thank you for your divine protection. I am so grateful that you are always assuring me.

Mighty God, I thank you for your Lordship, your power and your authority. Hallelujah. I pray in the mighty name of Jesus Christ.

Amen.

*Full scripture: Joshua 1:9 [Bible Citations: pg 218]

Thanksgiving for God's Promises

Isaiah 54:10: For the mountains shall depart, and the hills be removed; but my kindness shall not depart from thee, neither shall the covenant of my peace be removed, saith the LORD that hath mercy on thee.

Isaiah 40:29: He giveth power to the faint; and to them that have no might he increaseth strength.

Jeremiah 29:11: For I know the thoughts that I think toward you, saith the LORD, thoughts of peace, and not of evil, to give you an expected end.

Joshua 1:9: Have not I commanded thee? Be strong and of a good courage; be not afraid, neither be thou dismayed: for the LORD thy God is with thee whithersoever thou goest.

John 8:12: Then spake Jesus again unto them, saying, I am the light of the world: he that followeth me shall not walk in darkness, but shall have the light of life.

John 10:10: The thief cometh not, but for to steal, and to kill, and to destroy: I am come that they might have life, and that they might have it more abundantly.

James 1:5: If any of you lack wisdom, let him ask of God, that giveth to all men liberally and upbraideth not (without finding fault) and it shall be given him.

Mark 11:24: *Therefore I say unto you, what things soever ye desire, when ye pray, believe that ye receive them, and ye shall have them.*

Let us pray

Almighty God, your promises are sure, in **Psalm 119:105** *Thy word is a lamp unto our feet, and a light unto our path.* Mighty God, you gave me the light of your words to guide me and to give me assurance and confidence. Lord, these are words of hope and total trust. Father, I trust in you to perform your words in my life. If I walk in darkness I will stumble and fall, but if I walk in the light of your word, I shall stand as a towering lighthouse, to guide those who are in darkness to you. Hallelujah, praise God.

There are times when the mountain of darkness causes me to suffer health problems, financial problems, job problems, child problems, marital problems, and all different types of problems. These mountains of problems come to distract and to disappoint me. Lord, please let your Holy Spirit raise me up to embrace and to speak your words with power and authority against these mountains. I shall not be defeated for I am an overcomer in the name of Jesus Christ.

O Mighty God, please remind me to use the power of your word as my weapon to defeat every negative word of the enemy. Help me to speak your positive words to fight all my battles, for your promises are true and mighty. Hallelujah praise God! In the Mighty name of Jesus Christ, I pray.

Amen.

Some Meanings to Life

Happiness will keep me young and vibrant.

Trials will keep me strong and increase my faith in God.

Sorrows will keep me thinking like a human being.

Failures will keep me humble and dependable on God.

Challenges of life are normal for everyone.

But it is God who will keep us going forward.

Don't give up!

Don't give in!

Don't turn back!

Keep on going forward.

John 15:7: If ye abide in me, and my words abide in you, ye shall ask what ye will, and it shall be done unto you.

The word 'If' is a very important word. If we abide in Jesus Christ, and allow his word to abide in us, we can ask for His help, and it shall be done unto us. This promise is based on a condition. Let us abide in the word of God, and build a close relationship with him. This is a great opportunity to get great results when we ask anything of God according to his will.

Psalm 34:17-18. *¹⁷ The righteous cry, and the LORD heareth, and delivereth them out of all their troubles. ¹⁸ The LORD is nigh unto them that are of a broken heart; and saveth such as be of a contrite (crushed) spirit.*

Psalm 23:6: *Surely goodness and mercy shall follow me all the days of my life: and I will dwell in the house of the LORD forever.*

Let us pray

Sovereign God, I declare your word over my life and over the lives of my family.

I declare *John 15:7* over our lives. We are abiding in you and your words are abiding in us.

I declare *Psalm 34:17-18* over our lives. We will cry unto the Lord and he shall hear and deliver us from trouble.

I declare *Psalm 23:6* over our lives. We are sure that God's goodness and His mercies are following us all the days of our lives.

Lord, help us to keep your words in our heart, so that we will not sin against you.

Lord, we are in your classroom of learning. Help us to absorb your teachings and aim to pass every test.

Thank you Lord, for all your loving kindness towards us. In the Name of Jesus.

Amen.

Only God Knows the Real Me

PSALM 139:1-2

¹ O LORD, thou hast searched me, and known me. ² Thou knowest my downsitting and mine uprising, thou understandest my thought afar off.

LORD, only you know the real me. Only you know what is inside my heart. I am willing to accept change from a dark way of life to live in the light of your word. I understand that I cannot hide anything from you Lord, for all things are naked and open before you. I am weak but you are strong. I am limited but you are unlimited.

There are times when I am feeling low in spirit, lonely and hurting, but I am still smiling because you, Lord, are reassuring me. Sometimes I feel weak and vulnerable, and unable to defend myself, but you strengthen and comfort me. I position myself to meet with you every day. I raise my expectations to allow you to perform miracles of change in my life. I refuse to accommodate anything in my heart to depress me. I refuse to allow any thoughts of wickedness or negativity to enter into my heart. I lock the doors to selfishness. I refuse to accommodate any hatred or bitterness in my heart towards anyone.

I open up my heart's door for you to enter in, and to strengthen me. God, you has encouraged me to live in a loving relationship with you at all times. The Holy Spirit of God is always giving me a double portion of His anointing. God is helping me to be humble. I am committed to pray every day. I am willing to obey God, and He has made me to be the head and not the tail. God has made me to be above and not beneath.

I shall not live with regrets. I shall not lean on my own understanding but in all my life, I am willing to acknowledge the Lord, and depend on him to direct my path. I shall not allow failures to determine my future but I will rise up and start a new page in my life every day. I shall not be absent when I should be present. I shall not be eating when I should be fasting and praying. I shall not be sleeping when I should be awake. Because God has chosen me to do for himself.

Lord, I put my life into your nail scared hands, to lead me unto victory in the mighty name of Jesus.

Amen.

Believing in the True & Living God - Part 1

JOHN 1:1

In the beginning was the Word, and the Word was with God, and the Word was God.

I believe that the God of creation's name is Jesus Christ. The anointed One. I believe that there is no limitation in God the Father. He is the Lord of His creation and He is in control. Praise God.

The God of creation is described as follows:

Omnipresent
Meaning that He is everywhere.

Omnipotent
Meaning that He is all powerful.

Omniscient
Meaning that He is all-knowing and all seeing.

I believe that there is only **ONE GOD** of creation. He can be **who** and **what** He wants to be. He is in control. He has power over all things and at all times, and there is **NO God** beside Him.

I believe that there are no limitations in God. According to **John 4:24**: *God is a Spirit: and they that worship him must worship him in spirit and in truth.*

God is a Spirit. For me to have salvation He provided a human body to be the sacrifice for my sins. The name of this body is Jesus. *Matthew 1:21*: *says, And she shall bring forth a son and His name shall be called JESUS for He shall save His people from their sins.* When Jesus came to earth he was both human and divine.

Jesus is **THE** Christ, the anointed one. He was not only the son of God, or the son of David or the son of man, but he is the very God that came to earth in a human body, to save us from our sins with his own blood.

As a **human**, he was tired, and weary. He had emotions to cry. He became hungry for natural food so he ate and drank. However, as **Spirit**, He turned water into wine, healed the sick, raised the dead, calmed the sea and multiply fish and bread to fed hungry people. The body of Jesus was not eternal but His **Spirit** is eternal, is Divine. Hallelujah to Jesus.

According to *Philippians 2:10-11:* says: [10] *That at the name of Jesus every knee should bow, of things in heaven, and things in earth, and things under the earth;* [11] *And that every tongue should confess that Jesus Christ is Lord, to the glory of God the Father.*

John 1:10-12 says about Jesus: [10] *He was in the world, and the world was made by him, and the world knew him not.* [11] *He came unto his own, and his own received him not.* [12] *But as many as received him, to them He gave power to become the sons of God, even to them that believe on his name.*

I believe in Jesus Christ is Lord, He is the eternal God, and we receive salvation is in His name.

Hallelujah

Believing in the True & Living God - Part 2

God the Father He is the Holy Spirit, He called Jesus God: According to **Hebrews 1:8:** *⁑⁰ But unto the Son he saith, Thy throne, O God, is forever and ever: a sceptre of righteousness is the sceptre of thy kingdom.*

John 1:12: But as many as received him, to them gave he power to become the sons of God, even to them that believe on his name.

Acts 4:12: ¹⁰ Neither is there salvation in any other: for there is none other name under heaven given among men, whereby we must be saved.

The name of the Lord Jesus Christ is highly exalted, because His name is above every other name. ***Philippians 2:9-11*** says: *⁹ Wherefore God also hath highly exalted him, and give him a name which is above every name. ¹⁰ That at the name of Jesus every knee should bow, of things in heaven, and and things in the earth, and things under the earth; ¹¹ And that every tongue should confess that Jesus Christ is Lord, to the glory of God the Father.*

John 1:5: And the Light shineth in darkness; and the darkness comprehended it not.

This means that darkness couldn't understand or overpower the Light. Jesus Christ is that Light. For this reason, without the spiritual revelation about God, it is impossible for anyone to know or understand the mystery of God and his plan for salvation.

Let us pray

LORD, I believe that you are the true and living God, and there is no God beside you. Lord, only you can unlock your word through your Holy Spirit.

You are the one who opened the door of salvation for everyone to have a relationship with you. Lord, please fill us with your Holy Spirit that we can see you as Lord, as King and Redeemer.

Today I am determined, to live in total confidence and total trust in the Lord Jesus Christ, because by His stripes I am heal. Lord you are the only true and living God that can save and deliver me from the bondage of sin. Amen. Hallelujah.

Praise God. Hallelujah, Lord, you are a mighty God. Amen and Amen, praise God.

Amen.

By the Grace of God I Speak to my Body

Lord, by your grace, you gave me your Holy Spirit, I am in you and you are in me. I can ask for things that are according to your will, and you will give it unto me. Lord, according to your word, it is your will for me to have good health. Your word says I should ask and I will receive, seek and I will find, knock and the door shall be open. **(Matthew 7:7)**

Today I am speaking to my body. I command it to line up with your word. I speak to every tissue, every organ of my body to receive the word of God and produce good health. I command my body to function in perfection, and operate just as God has created it to function. I speak to every blood vessel, every bone and muscle of my body to function well, and to line up with the word of God, so I can live in good health. I speak to my brain cells, my memory cells to be renewed and restored in the mighty name of Jesus Christ of Nazareth.

I forbid any type of sickness or disease to operate in my body, for my body is the temple of the living God. My body is God's dwelling place. I am the winner of every battle because the weapons of my warfare are not carnal, but they are mighty through God to the pulling down of strongholds.

According to **2 Corinthians 10:5*,** I am casting down every imagination and every high thing that exalts itself against the knowledge of God, and I am bringing into captivity every thought, to the obedience of Christ. By the grace of God, I take authority over ever-false imagination that wants to confuse my mind and to torment me. By the grace of God, I believe that the Holy Spirit of God is active in my body. The power of God's word is taking active force in my life right now, to destroy everything that wants to put me into captivity against the obedience of God.

Let us pray

I worship you Lord Jesus, with confidence I declare my healing. I live by faith and not by sight. No good thing will be withheld from me when I am walking upright. Lord Jesus Christ, you has delivered me from slavery, captivity and from every form of bondage.

Lord, I thank you so much that you have appointed and positioned me for greatness. I shall receive benefits and blessings every day of my life.

I bow down my knees to worship you, O Lord; I adore you, for you are my God. Father, I love you with my whole heart, and I will serve you all the days of my life. Amen and Amen.

Lord, I thank you for honouring these declarations over my body; I thank you for hearing and answering my prayers.

Amen.

*Full scripture: 2 Corinthians 10:5 [Bible Citations: pg 218]

Saying a Prayer Before we Eat Our Meals

Exodus 23:25

And ye shall serve the LORD your God,
and he shall bless thy bread, and thy water;
and I will take away sickness from the midst of thee.

On your own

Lord, I thank you for this meal. I pray that you will bless it and sanctify it, that it will do good for my body in Jesus name. **Amen.**

O Lord my God, I thank you for this meal that I am about to eat. Lord, I am conscious that you have provided it for me. I pray that you will bless it, that it will nurture my body.
In the name of Jesus, I pray. Amen.

With family and friends

Father God, we are so grateful to you for providing this meal for us today. You provide our daily bread and we are satisfied. Lord, we are also aware that there are people who go hungry. We are willing to share what we have with them.
Father, we ask that you bless this meal in the name of Jesus. Amen.

Merciful Father, we thank you for providing this meal for us. We thank you for blessing our bread and our water, so that it will nurture our bodies. Lord, we are grateful for your kindness towards us.
In the name of Jesus, we pray. Amen.

Dear Lord, we thank you for this meal. We pray that you will bless it, and sanctify it. Lord, please take out every impurity so that it will bring healing and strength to our bodies.
In the name of Jesus, we pray. Amen.

Lord, we thank you for this meal that you have provided, we pray that you will bless it. Bless the hands that have prepared it, and bless the source that it has come from.
In the name of Jesus, we pray. Amen.

Declarations by Faith

Declarations by Faith - Part 1

AS I wake up this morning, I have activated my faith by the anointing power of the Holy Spirit of God. Today, I am sitting in the classroom of the Lord and He is teaching me all that I need to know about his word, what I need to do, and how I can be prosperous in life. I believe that my prosperity is not in man's power, but in the power of the Lord God Almighty.

By faith, I declare that God's love is growing stronger and stronger inside me. This morning I am receiving the supernatural power of God. I will face my day with confidence and nothing shall stand in my way.

I declare **Psalm 118:17:** over my life- *I shall not die, but live, and declare the works of the Lord.*

I am receiving an abundance of grace, to pray, to take courage and blessings from my God. I declare salvation over the nations that everyone will surrender to their creator.

By the grace of God. I declare that I am generous and tender hearted. I am willing to help those who are in need, just as God has commanded me to do.

By the grace of God, I shall not be a deceiver. I shall not treat anyone with injustice or partiality. I shall not seek to mislead anyone. I am committed to be honest, faithful and forgiving. My desire is to do that which is right and pleasing in the sight of God.

With the help of God, I declare that I shall live in the peace of God. According to **John 14:27** Jesus said: *Peace I leave with you, my peace*

I give unto you: not as the world giveth, give I unto you. Let not your heart be troubled, neither let it be afraid. I declare that the peace of God is giving me calmness and tranquillity in my everyday circumstances of my life. I declare that I am receiving courage and strength from God to face every challenge because His perfect peace is living inside of me.

By the grace of God, I declare that nothing shall rob me of anything that God has provide for me. God has given me the ability and power to maintain His wonderful gift of peace. This kind of peace comes directly from the Lord Jesus Christ to me. I will always value the heavenly treasures that is in the peace of God. Thank you Jesus.

As a wife, I will love, respect and care for my husband and my family, according to **Proverbs 31:10-31***. I am committed to sit in the classroom of a virtuous woman. I am learning the values of life. I am committed to fasting and prayer following the examples of Jesus. I will read the word of God and seek to live by them. I will serve my family and those who are in need of help; I will be generous.

As a husband, I am committed to love, respect and care for my wife and family, just as Christ has commanded me. I am committed to pray, read the word of God and to live a holy life, and I will lead my family into prayer every day.

Amen.

*Full scripture: Proverbs 31: 10-31 [Bible Citations: pg 212]

Declarations by Faith - Part 2

By faith, I declare over my life *Philippians 1:6: Being: confident of this very thing, that He which hath began a good work in you will perform it until the day of Jesus Christ.*

With all confidence, I believe that God, who has begun a good work in me, and you are capable to complete it, until the day of Jesus Christ. Glory to the Most High God.

I speak *Philippians 2:13: For it is God which worketh in you both to will and to do of his good pleasure.* I declare the power of this word over my life that it is God's will to do his good pleasure in me and through me.

I declare the peace of God according to *Philippians 4:7: And the peace of God, which passeth all understanding, shall keep your hearts and minds through Christ Jesus.* Right now, I am residing in the perfect peace of God. I may not understand how it works, but it is all about God. He is keeping my heart and my mind in His perfect peace.

According to *Philippians 3:13-14*,* I am forgetting those things which are behind me, and I am reaching forward to those things which are ahead. I am pressing towards the goal, for the prize of the high calling in Christ Jesus.

Let us pray

Lord, you have chosen me for yourself as a special treasure, and I am bless beyond measure. By your grace, I shall always have something to give to those who are in need, I shall always be the lender and not the borrower.

According to **Deuteronomy 28:6*,** I am blessed when I come in, and blessed when I go out. I receive these words in the mighty name of Jesus. According to **Hebrews 13:8:** *Jesus Christ the same yesterday, today and forever.* Lord Jesus Christ you are downloading your divine favours into my life every day. Let the fragrance of the aroma of your love strengthen me.

Jesus Christ you can do anything and everything, except fail. Your unconditional love for me is excelling and increasing in my life every day. My God, you will never fail me or forsake me. I look forward to hearing your voice early in the morning and throughout the day. Jesus Christ you are the core of my life, and I am in fellowship with you, Mighty God your Holy Spirit has built a firewall of protection around me.

I declare that according to **Psalm 23:6:** *Surely, goodness and mercy shall follow me, all the days of my life: and I will dwell in the house of the LORD forever.* Lord I am sure that your goodness and mercy is with me. Praise God.

Glory Hallelujah. Praise God. Praise God.

*Full scripture: Philippians 3:13-14:
Deuteronomy 28:6: [Bible Citations: pg 218]

Declarations by Faith - Part 3

By my faith and by the grace of God, I declare the following over my life:

I am blessed and not cursed; Jesus has removed the curse from me.

I am above and not beneath.

I am healthy and not sick.

I am the righteousness of God, in Christ Jesus.

I am an overcomer, and a conqueror by the blood of Jesus Christ.

I am a child of God. I am free and not bound. I live in good courage.

I am handpicked by God.

I am the head and not the tail, I am above and not beneath

I am baptised in the name of Jesus Christ for the remission of my sins.

I am waiting for the return of the Lord Jesus Christ.

I am a true worshiper for God.

I walk in victory and not in defeat, I think positive and sober.

I walk by faith and not by sight, because God has made me to be a light in this dark world.

I will always remember that life without struggle is a life without success.

I will not give up, I will not quit, but I will go forward in Jesus name.

I shall not allow my emotions to dominate my life and bring me into captivity.

I shall not allow my past to block my future. I am unstoppable.

I shall live in total happiness and not in distress or confusion.

I am more than a conqueror through Christ that loved me. **Romans 8:37-39***

I am planted by the rivers of water.

I shall bring forth fruits in its season.

My leaf shall not wither: and whatsoever I do shall prosper.

I will only speak positive words over my life, because I am a child of God.

I will always speak the truth.

I will bless Israel, and blessings shall come back to me.

I will show love, mercy and compassion to all, and it shall come back to me.

I receive the gift of the holy spirit of God according to the Holy Scripture.

I am a wise child of God, and I shall make a difference wherever I go.

I reverse every negative word that anyone may speak against my family or me.

I seek the wisdom of God to lead me into victory at all times.

I speak peace, healing and prosperity over my life.

I shall not live in worry, because God is taking care of my situation. **Hallelujah.**

Declarations by Faith - Part 4

I shall not do anything that will cause my family or me shame.

I speak against the spirit of adultery and sexual perversion.

I shall not put anything in my body to hurt me or to make me sick.

I speak against illegal drugs, alcoholism and every kind of addiction.

I speak against every evil spirit that may want to attack my family or me. God has given me the authority to send them back to the pit of hell, by the blood of Jesus.

I shall not be held captive by the forces of any form of bondage.

I command every deception barrier to come down in the name of Jesus.

I shall work and spend my money wisely.

I shall always give generously of my time, money and prayers just as God commands me to give to those who are in need.

I shall live in the place of God's blessings at all times.

I shall read and meditate on the word of God with confidence in Him.

I am planted by the rivers of water, and I shall bring forth fruits in its season. My leaves shall not wither and whatsoever I do shall always prosper.

I believe that the word of God is true, and by the grace of God, I will follow the commands of Jesus Christ my Lord.

I believe that God is able to empower me, with all spiritual abilities by the actions of fasting and prayer.

I purpose in my heart that I will follow the actions of Jesus Christ in prayer, just as He left an example for us to follow.

I will use the word of God to overcome and defeat every attack of the enemy. According to ***Matthew 4:4*** Jesus said: *But he answered and said, It is written, Man shall not live by bread alone, but by every word that proceedeth out of the mouth of God.*

Psalm 118:17: *I shall not die, but live and declare the works of the Lord.*

With the help of God, I will allow God's Holy Spirit to lead me into prayer, so that as I make my petitions known unto him, He will hear and answer me.

Challenges may come but they will cause me to be more responsible, to be stronger and more alert, for God is by my side.

Hallelujah.

Declarations by Faith - Part 5

BY the leading of the Holy Spirit of God, I will use scriptural references and quotations to strengthen me in prayer; I shall receive divine revelations to open doors of spiritual visions and opportunities for the glory of God.

I depend on the Holy Spirit of God to intervene on my behalf at all times. I understand that prayer is one of God's powerful guidelines that will allow me to have a more intimate relationship with Him, and through prayer God will help me to live a more meaningful and peaceful lifestyle and receive His revelation.

I declare that my life shall live in the fruit of the Spirit, according to **Galatians 5:22:** [22] *But the fruit of the Spirit is love, joy, peace, long-suffering, gentleness, goodness, faith:* [23]*Meekness, temperance: against such there is no law (or restrictions).*

I am willing to bear fruits for the Lord to receive a good harvest. I am in God's waiting room so that I will learn how to produce these characteristics. I am aware that God may use some people and different types of experiences to shape my life. By the grace of God, I declare that I will pass every test for the glory of God.

By the grace of God, I speak to my mind to adjust to God's divine word. My faith shall increase in God's love. I will continue to trust in God's words concerning my life. I declare that I will serve in His ministry. I declare that God has given me the authority to speak against every situation that may want to come to attack my body to stop my purpose. I speak against sickness, disease, virus, problems and issues of every kind. I am victorious in the Mighty name of Jesus Christ.

I believe that when I pray, God hears and answers my petitions. I believe that God will always change situations and grant me favours. I am committed that God's grace is capable to help me to perform and fulfil my goals with confidence for his glory.

God has appointed and anointed me to have self-control so that I can fulfil His purpose for His glory. God has empowered me and inspired me to succeed in life. God has put a fence around me and I am safe and secure.

I declare that My God is the King of glory. He is controlling my life. I refuse to allow anyone to oppress me or to block me from my relationship with Him. God is guiding and teaching me. God is leading me in the right direction to receive my inheritance.

I trust in God, I believe His word. I am meditating on His word day and night. I declare that God's word is my daily bread and my water.

Today I live in total confidence in God; I am trusting in the mighty name of the Lord Jesus Christ.

Hallelujah.

A Selection of Bible Verses of God's Promises

Matthew 1:21: And she shall bring forth a son, and thou shalt call his name Jesus: for he shall save his people from their sins.

Matthew 7:7-8: [7] Ask, and it shall be given you; seek, and ye shall find; knock, and it shall be opened unto you. [8] For every one that asketh receiveth; and he that seeketh findeth; and to him that knocketh it shall be opened.

1 John 5:14-15: [14] And this is the confidence that we have in Him, that, if we ask anything according to His will, He heareth us. [15] And if we know that He hear us, whatsoever we ask, we know that we have the petitions that we desired of Him.

Psalm 55:22: Cast your burden upon the LORD, and He shall sustain thee: He shall never suffer the righteous to be moved.

John 16:33: These things I have spoken unto you, in me ye might have peace. In the world ye shall have tribulation: But be of good cheer, I have overcome the world.

3 John 1:2: Beloved, I wish above all things that thou mayest prosper and be in health, even as thy soul prospereth.

Jeremiah 29:11: For I know the thoughts that I think towards you, saith the LORD, thoughts of peace, and not of evil, to give you an expected end.

1 John 1:9: *If we confess our sins, He is faithful and just to forgive us our sins, and to cleanse us from all unrighteousness.*

Lord, I am depending on your word to sustain me, because your word is a life- giving stream for my daily survival. Praise God.

Hallelujah.

A Selection of Bible Verses Referring to Jesus

John 11:25-26: [25] *Jesus said unto her, I am the resurrection and the life: he that believeth in me though he were dead, yet shall he live.* [26] *And whosoever liveth and believeth in me shall never die. Believest thou this?*

Acts 4:12: *Neither is there salvation in any other: for there is none other name under heaven given among men, whereby we must be saved.*

Colossians 3:17: *And whatsoever ye do in word or deed, do all in the name of the Lord Jesus, giving thanks to God and the Father by him.*

John 14:6: *Jesus saith unto him, I am the way, the truth, and the life: no man cometh unto the Father, but by me.*

John 14:13: *And whatsoever ye shall ask in my name, that will I do, that the Father may be glorified in the Son.*

Romans 10:13: *For whosoever shall call upon the name of the Lord shall be saved.*

Matthew 28:19: *Go ye therefore, and teach all nations, baptising them in the name of the Father, and of the Son and of the Holy Ghost.*

Acts 2:38: *Then Peter said unto them, Repent, and be baptised every one of you in the name of Jesus Christ for the remission of sins, and ye shall receive the gift of the Holy Ghost.*

The God of creation: His name is Jesus Christ. *John 5:43 Jesus said I am come in my Father's name and ye receive me not: if another shall come in his own name, him ye will receive.*

The name of Jesus **is above every other name. His name is eternal, mighty, powerful, Holy and righteous. By Faith, we use The Name of Jesus to receive help.**

Colossians 3:17 **says:** *And whatsoever ye do in word or deed, do all in the name of Jesus.*

Hallelujah.

Remember that **GOD is in Control**

Remember that God is in Control

THE kindness that you give today, may not always be the same thing you get back in return; sometimes more, sometimes less, sometimes worse and sometimes you get none at all. But remember that the Lord said in **Acts 20:35:** *I have shewed you all things, how that so labouring ye ought to support the weak, and to remember the words of the Lord Jesus, how he said, It is more* **blessed to give** *than to receive.* Never forget to give with a loving heart, for God will reward you. Praise God

REMEMBER TO TRUST IN THE LORD!

Trust in the Lord and believe in His name. He is able to remove all your pains, sadness, worries, problems, difficulties and anxieties. God is capable to replace them with good health, peace, love, happiness and blessings in abundance. Praise God.

Remember the benefit of the church – is to be a partaker of God's kingdom.

If you are a part of the church of the living God, there is hope for you. If you have not started yet, let me encourage you to come to the Lord Jesus Christ. Everyone is welcome. You will be safe and secure in Jesus Christ. Jesus said he will build his church and the Gates of hell shall not prevail against it. If we are in the church of Jesus Christ, He is well capable to sustain us.

Remember that no one shall be able to take us out of the hand of God. We are established in righteousness, and we have authority to use the word of God to cancel every assignment of the enemies.

Remember that we are overcomers by the blood of the lamb (Jesus) by the word of our testimony. Hallelujah. Hallelujah to Jesus Christ our saviour. Amen.

Remember-*Romans 8:35, 37-39:* *³⁵ Who shall separate us from the love of Christ? Shall tribulation, or distress, or persecution, or famine, or nakedness, or peril, or sword? ³⁷ Nay, in all these things we are more than conquerors through him that loved us. ³⁸ For I am persuaded, that neither death, nor life, nor angels, nor principalities, nor powers, nor things present, nor things to come, ³⁹ Nor height, nor depth, nor any other creature, shall be able to separate us from the love of God, which is in Christ Jesus our Lord.*

Let nothing or no one separate us from the love of God.

Remember that - Jesus have redeemed us, and has set us free; He carried all sickness and all disease in His own body. He suffered on Calvary, so that we can be healed. He didn't do this for one person, but for the whole world. Thank you Lord.

Blessings

NUMBERS 6:24-26

[24] The LORD bless thee, and keep thee: [25] The LORD make His face to shine upon thee, and be gracious unto thee: [26] The LORD lift up His countenance upon thee, and give thee peace.

2 CORINTHIANS 13:14

The grace of our LORD Jesus Christ, and the love of God, and the communion of the Holy Ghost, be with you all. Amen.

Ephesians 3:20-21: [20] Now unto Him that is able to do exceeding abundantly above all that we ask or think, according to the power that worketh in us. [21] Unto Him be glory in the church by Jesus Christ throughout all ages, world without end. Amen.

Jude 24-25: [24] Now unto Him that is able to keep you from falling, and to present you faultless before the presence of His glory with exceeding joy. [25] To the only wise God our saviour, be glory and majesty, dominion and power, both now and ever. Amen.

Philemon 1:25: The grace of our Lord Jesus Christ be with your spirit. Amen.

Matthew 5:6: Blessed are they which do hunger and thirst after righteousness: for they shall be filled.

Matthew 5:9: *Blessed are the peacemakers: for they shall be called the children of God.*

Matthew 5:11-12: *[11] blessed are ye when men shall revile, you and persecute you and shall say all manner of evil against you falsely, for my sake: [12] Rejoice and be exceedingly glad: for great is your reward in heaven: for so persecuted the prophets which were before you.*

1 Corinthians 2:9: *But it is written, Eye have not seen, nor ear heard, neither have entered into the heart of man, the things which God hath prepared for them that love him.*

And now, may the saving grace of our Lord and Saviour Jesus Christ, the love of God, the faithful fellowship of the Holy Spirit, the Comfort, rest, remain and abide with us all, both now and for ever more. Hallelujah.

Amen.

Conclusion

IT IS TIME TO PRAY, PRAYER BOOK

The author was inspired to write this prayer book, and with help of the Holy Spirit of God, she obeyed.

The author had many different kinds of experience and many different challenges as she wrote this prayer book. The author understands that it is natural that when we are committed to do something for the Lord, the enemy will always turn up with a package to bring confusion, frustration and discouragements.

In *Matthew 7:24-27,* Jesus likened everyone who obeyed his words, to a wise man who built his house upon the rock. When the rain descended and the floods came, and the wind blew and beat upon that house, it fell not; for it was founded upon the rock.

Those who disobey His word he likened them to a foolish man who built his house upon the sand. When the rain descended, and the wind blew and beat upon that house, it fell, and great was the fall of it.

This teaches us that if we obey God's word, our foundation will be stable and strong, but if we do not, our foundation will be weak and crumble. Let us obey the word of God, regardless of the challenges that we encounter in life.

Acknowledgements

First of all, I would like to give thanks to the Lord Jesus Christ, who has enlightened and strengthened me all the way, as I wrote this prayer book. The Lord has journeyed with me night and day. He inspired me and encouraged me; He strengthened me with his words. I found hope and confidence in the Lord. I give all the glory and all the honour to the Most High God.

Many thanks to my dear mother Mrs Viola Gordon, who taught her children how to read the bible. She taught us that it is very important to pray to the true and living God, Jesus Christ our Lord and saviour.

Special thanks to my family, for their patience and support, especially my brother Wesley and my son Aldene, during the times that I spent writing this prayer book. It is always a privilege to share my life with my families; they understood my dedication to this project.

Many thanks to my niece Carol who spent quality time with me, to proofread my book. I give thanks to God for her understanding, courage and patience with me.

Many thanks to my niece Angela for sharing quality time with me and for her encouragement. She generously assisted with the design of my book, making sure it met a high standard.

I declare God's blessings upon our lives in the name of Jesus.

I really appreciate all your help. God is a real way maker. Praise God. We give all the glory and the entire honour to you Lord Jesus.

About The Author

SYLVIA SAMMS is a true believer in Jesus Christ. She has received the revelation that there is only one God, and through His name we receive salvation. According to *Acts 4:12*: *Neither is there salvation in any other: for there is none other name under heaven given among men, whereby we must be saved.*

Sylvia was baptised in the name of Jesus Christ, on the island of Jamaica in the Bethel Apostolic Church of Jesus Christ on the 6th January 1978.

Since that time, the grace of God has been sustaining her in the faith. She has been filled with the Holy Spirit and is always willing to serve in the ministry. She is always willing to help other people as much as she can. She has experienced many challenges in her life, and based on her own personal experiences, when she prays she has received help from the Lord.

Sylvia believes that prayer is one of the most powerful keys that God has given to every one of us to use, to receive help from Him. There were times in her life when she was going through health problems, depression, deprivation, homelessness, and marital problems (just to mention a few). Sylvia cried out to the Lord in prayer and fasting. God helped her and changed her situation for the better.

She continued to experience the love of God embracing and comforting her. She found strength and courage, and she found love and security in the Lord Jesus Christ. With the help of God, Sylvia is committed to prayer and to seek God for his daily help. She has received healing for herself many times. When she has prayed for others, many have also received healing, strength and courage by the supernatural power of God.

Sylvia serves as an Evangelist in the church that she is now attending in the UK. She graduated in October 2018 after completing her bible studies with the Bethel Institute of Biblical Studies. Her faith in the Lord allowed her to give hope to many people through phone calls and on social media prayer lines. She is a regular gospel presenter on a local radio station serving the community.

In the year 2020, she was inspired to write this prayer book, and to name it: **IT IS TIME TO PRAY.** Her aim is to motivate people to pray, and to seek God's help and gain confidence in the Lord Jesus Christ.

Prayer helps Sylvia in difficult times, and she believes that it will do the same for others. Sylvia also believes that prayer is a good way to build a relationship with God.

You are encouraged to pray, not only for yourself but also for others, and you will experience spiritual changes. As you read this prayer book, believe in God. For whatever you are asking Him for, wait on Him to accomplish it.

Read this prayer book, trusting and depending on God for your healing and protection. Ask God for financial help and everything that you need. He will listen and help you. There are no limitations in God, just believe that He is well able and capable to meet all your needs and watch Him work for you. Read this prayer book and declare the words of faith over your life and over you family's life.

Sylvia has had many different types of experience of God helping her when she prays. Prayer works for her every time and the words of God are very powerful over her life.

May the Lord Jesus Christ bless you and your family and keep you all in his care always. God is able to protect and defend you at all times.

Psalm 118:8: *It is better to trust in the Lord than to put confidence in man.*

Psalm 118:1: *O give thanks unto the Lord; for He is good: because His mercy endureth forever.*

Psalm 34:15: *The eyes of the Lord are upon the righteous, and His ears are open unto their cry.*

Psalm 19:14*: Let the words of my mouth and the meditation of my heart, be acceptable in thy sight, O Lord, my strength, and my redeemer.*

Romans 8:28: *And we know that all things work together for good to them that love God, to them who are the called according to his purpose.*

Blessed and Holy is the name of the LORD. Hallelujah.

Analysing

The author had much challenges writing this prayer book. However, with much determination, she was persistent, committed and willing to complete this blessed prayer book. By the leading of the Holy Spirit of God.

The author's aim was to finish the assignment that God has given her to do, she believes that the readers will receive great benefits when they read this powerful prayer book.

Achievements

The Author worked alongside the Publisher Tarnya, her two nieces Angela and Carol, and with the leading of the Holy Spirit of God, the prayer book was completed. All the honour, praise and glory goes to the Almighty God. Teamwork will make the dream work. Praise God!

Encouragements

Let us be encouraged that we can achieve much, if the foundation of our faith is strong in the Lord, and we are willing to work hard in unity.

Praise and honour to the Most High God.

***Psalm 103:1-5** [1] Bless the LORD O my soul: and all that is within me bless his holy name. [2] Bless the LORD, O my soul, and forget not all* *his benefits: ³ Who forgiveth all thine iniquities; who heal all thy diseases: ⁴ Who redeemeth thy life from destruction; who crowneth thee with loving kindness and tender mercies; ⁵ Who satisfieth thy mouth with good things; so that thy youth is renewed like the eagles.*

Amen and Amen.

Bibliography

The inspiration for the declarations and prayers in this prayer book came from the Holy Spirit working in and through the author.

The quotations in this prayer book may read differently to those in other versions of the bible, so please feel free to use your own bible for the words you are more familiar with.

PHILIPPIANS 4:13

I can do all things through Christ
which strengtheneth me.

There is life in the word of God!

Read and be blessed.

Amen

Bible Citations

Page 2- *Ephesians 4:22-32*
[22] That ye put off concerning the former conversation the old man, which is corrupt according to the deceitful lusts; [23] And be renewed in the spirit of your mind; [24] And that ye put on the new man, which after God is created in righteousness and true holiness. [25] Wherefore putting away lying, speak every man truth with his neighbour: for we are members one of another. [26] Be ye angry, and sin not: let not the sun go down upon your wrath: [27] Neither give place to the devil. [28] Let him that stole steal no more: but rather let him labour, working with his hands the thing which is good, that he may have to give to him that needeth. [29] Let no corrupt communication proceed out of your mouth, but that which is good to the use of edifying, that it may minister grace unto the hearers. [30] And grieve not the Holy Spirit of God, whereby ye are sealed unto the day of redemption. [31] Let all bitterness, and wrath, and anger, and clamour, and evil speaking, be put away from you, with all malice: [32] And be ye kind one to another, tender-hearted, forgiving one another, even as God for Christ's sake hath forgiven you.

Page 28- *Luke 18:1*
And he spake a parable unto them to this end, that men ought always to pray, and not to faint;

Page 33- *Genesis 12:3*
And I will bless them that bless thee, and curse him that curseth thee: and in thee shall all families of the earth be blessed.

Page 37- Psalm 1:3
And he shall be like a tree planted by the rivers of water, that bringeth forth his fruit in his season; his leaf also shall not wither; and whatsoever he doeth shall prosper.

Page 37- Jude 24-25
[24] Now unto him that is able to keep you from falling, and to present you faultless before the presence of his glory with exceeding joy [25] To the only wise God our Saviour, be glory and majesty, dominion and power, both now and ever. Amen.

Page 37- John 15:7
If ye abide in me, and my words abide in you, ye shall ask what ye will, and it shall be done unto you.

Page 39- Psalm 107:20
He sent his word, and healed them, and delivered them from their destructions.

Page 39- Isaiah 53:5
But He was wounded for our transgressions, He was bruised for our iniquities: the chastisement of our peace was upon Him; and with His stripes we are healed.

Page 41- Philippians 1:6
Being confident of this very thing, that He which hath begun a good work in you will perform it until the day of Jesus Christ.

Page 49- 1 Peter 5:2-4
[2] Feed the flock of God which is among you, taking the oversight thereof, not by constraint, but willingly; not for filthy lucre, but of a ready mind; [3] Neither as being lords over God's heritage, but being examples to the flock. [4] And when the chief Shepherd shall appear, ye shall receive a crown of glory that fadeth not away.

Page 51- 1 Timothy 2:1
I exhort therefore, that, first of all, supplications, prayers, intercessions, and giving of thanks, be made for all men.

Page 59- Jeremiah 29:11
For I know the thoughts that I think toward you, saith the Lord, thoughts of peace, and not of evil, to give you an expected end.

Page 67- Psalm 41:4
I said, Lord, be merciful unto me: heal my soul; for I have sinned against thee.

Page 67- Isaiah 41:10
Fear thou not; for I am with thee: be not dismayed; for I am thy God: I will strengthen thee; yea, I will help thee; yea, I will uphold thee with the right hand of my righteousness.

Page 67- Jeremiah 17:14
Heal me, O Lord, and I shall be healed; save me, and I shall be saved: for thou art my praise.

Page 67- Jeremiah 30:17
For I will restore health unto thee, and I will heal thee of thy wounds, saith the Lord; because they called thee an Outcast, saying, This is Zion, whom no man seeketh after.

Page 67- Mark 5:34
And He said unto her, Daughter, thy faith hath made thee whole; go in peace, and be whole of thy plague.

Page 67- Philippians 4:19
But my God shall supply all your need according to his riches in glory by Christ Jesus.

Page 67- Revelations 21:4
And God shall wipe away all tears from their eyes; and there shall be no more death, neither sorrow, nor crying, neither shall there be any more pain: for the former things are passed away.

Page 72- Isaiah 64:8
But now, O Lord, thou art our father; we are the clay, and thou our potter; and we are the work of thy hand.

Page 74- Deuteronomy 6:4-9
[4] Hear, O Israel: The Lord our God is one Lord: [5] And thou shalt love the Lord thy God with all thine heart, and with all thy soul, and with all thy might. [6] And these words, which I command thee this day, shall be in thine heart: [7] And thou shalt teach them diligently unto thy children, and shalt talk of them when thou sittest in thine house, and when thou walkest by the way, and when thou liest down, and when thou risest up. [8] And thou shalt bind them for a sign upon thine hand, and they shall be as frontlets between thine eyes. [9] And thou shalt write them upon the posts of thy house, and on thy gates.

Page 79- Isaiah 26:3
Thou wilt keep him in perfect peace, whose mind is stayed on thee: because he trusteth in thee.

Page 81- Psalm 119:165
Great peace have they which love thy law: and nothing shall offend them.

Page 81- Psalm 34:14
Depart from evil, and do good; seek peace, and pursue it.

Page 81- Romans 16:20
And the God of peace shall bruise Satan under your feet shortly. The grace of our Lord Jesus Christ be with you. Amen.

Page 81- Philippians 4:7
And the peace of God, which passeth all understanding, shall keep your hearts and minds through Christ Jesus.

Page 83- Psalm 4:8
I will both lay me down in peace, and sleep: for thou, Lord, only makest me dwell in safety.

Page 83- 2 Thessalonians 3:16
Now the Lord of peace himself give you peace always by all means. The Lord be with you all.

Page 83- Galatians 5:22
But the fruit of the Spirit is love, joy, peace, longsuffering, gentleness, goodness, faith.

Page 89- Hebrews 10:16
This is the covenant that I will make with them after those days, saith the Lord, I will put my laws into their hearts, and in their minds will I write them;

Page 96- Psalm 107:20
He sent his word, and healed them, and delivered them from their destructions.

Page 96- Psalm 147:3
He healeth the broken in heart, and bindeth up their wounds.

Page 101- 2 Timothy 1:7
For God hath not given us the spirit of fear; but of power, and of love, and of a sound mind.

Page 101- Romans 8:28
And we know that all things work together for good to them that love God, to them who are the called according to his purpose.

Page 108- Acts 2:41
Then they that gladly received His word were baptised: and the same day there were added unto them about three thousand souls.

Page 110- Acts 5:3
But Peter said, Ananias, why hath Satan filled thine heart to lie to the Holy Ghost, and to keep back part of the price of the land?

Page 110- Acts 5:9-10
⁹ Then Peter said unto her, How is it that ye have agreed together to tempt the Spirit of the Lord? Behold, the feet of them which have buried thy husband are at the door, and shall carry thee out. ¹⁰ Then fell she down straightway at his feet, and yielded up the ghost: and the young men came in, and found her dead, and, carrying her forth, buried her by her husband.

Page 110- Acts 16:18
And this did she many days. But Paul, being grieved, turned and said to the spirit, I command thee in the name of Jesus Christ to come out of her. And he came out the same hour.

Page 113- 1 Timothy 2:1-2
¹ I exhort therefore, that, first of all, supplications, prayers, intercessions, and giving of thanks, be made for all men; ² For kings, and for all that are in authority; that we may lead a quiet and peaceable life in all godliness and honesty.

Page 118- Deuteronomy 31:6
Be strong and of a good courage, fear not, nor be afraid of them: for the Lord thy God, He it is that doth go with thee; He will not fail thee, nor forsake thee.

Page 124- 1 Corinthians 7:3

Let the husband render unto the wife due benevolence: and likewise also the wife unto the husband.

Page 130- Ephesians 5: 22-33

[22] Wives, submit yourselves unto your own husbands, as unto the Lord. [23] For the husband is the head of the wife, even as Christ is the head of the church: and he is the saviour of the body. [24] Therefore as the church is subject unto Christ, so let the wives be to their own husbands in every thing. [25] Husbands, love your wives, even as Christ also loved the church, and gave himself for it; [26] That He might sanctify and cleanse it with the washing of water by the word, [27] That He might present it to himself a glorious church, not having spot, or wrinkle, or any such thing; but that it should be holy and without blemish. [28] So ought men to love their wives as their own bodies. He that loveth his wife loveth himself. [29] For no man ever yet hated his own flesh; but nourisheth and cherisheth it, even as the Lord the church: [30] For we are members of His body, of His flesh, and of His bones. [31] For this cause shall a man leave his father and mother, and shall be joined unto his wife, and they two shall be one flesh. [32] This is a great mystery: but I speak concerning Christ and the church. [33] Nevertheless let every one of you in particular so love his wife even as himself; and the wife see that she reverence her husband.

Page 134 Proverbs 31:10-31

[10] Who can find a virtuous woman? For her price is far above rubies. [11] The heart of her husband doth safely trust in her, so that he shall have no need of spoil. [12] She will do him good and not evil all the days of her life. [13] She seeketh wool, and flax, and worketh willingly with her hands. [14] She is like the merchants 'ships; she bringeth her food from afar. [15] She riseth also while it is yet night, and giveth meat to her household, and a portion to her maidens. [16] She considereth a field,

and buyeth it: with the fruit of her hands she planteth a vineyard.[17] She girdeth her loins with strength, and strengtheneth her arms.[18] She perceiveth that her merchandise is good: her candle goeth not out by night.[19] She layeth her hands to the spindle, and her hands hold the distaff.[20] She stretcheth out her hand to the poor; yea, she reacheth forth her hands to the needy.[21] She is not afraid of the snow for her household: for all her household are clothed with scarlet.[22] She maketh herself coverings of tapestry; her clothing is silk and purple.[23] Her husband is known in the gates, when he sitteth among the elders of the land.[24] She maketh fine linen, and selleth it; and delivereth girdles unto the merchant.[25] Strength and honour are her clothing; and she shall rejoice in time to come.[26] She openeth her mouth with wisdom; and in her tongue is the law of kindness.[27] She looketh well to the ways of her household, and eateth not the bread of idleness.[28] Her children arise up, and call her blessed; her husband also, and he praiseth her.[29] Many daughters have done virtuously, but thou excellest them all.[30] Favour is deceitful, and beauty is vain: but a woman that feareth the Lord, she shall be praised.[31] Give her of the fruit of her hands; and let her own works praise her in the gates.

Page 138- Isaiah 54:17
No weapon that is formed against thee shall prosper; and every tongue that shall rise against thee in judgment thou shalt condemn. This is the heritage of the servants of the Lord, and their righteousness is of me, saith the Lord.

Page 138- Psalm 23:4
Yea, though I walk through the valley of the shadow of death, I will fear no evil: for thou art with me; thy rod and thy staff they comfort me.

Page 140- Ephesians 6:10-17

10 Finally, my brethren, be strong in the Lord, and in the power of His might. *11* Put on the whole armour of God, that ye may be able to stand against the wiles of the devil. *12* For we wrestle not against flesh and blood, but against principalities, against powers, against the rulers of the darkness of this world, against spiritual wickedness in high places. *13* Wherefore take unto you the whole armour of God, that ye may be able to withstand in the evil day, and having done all, to stand. *14* Stand therefore, having your loins girt about with truth, and having on the breastplate of righteousness; *15* And your feet shod with the preparation of the gospel of peace; *16*Above all, taking the shield of faith, wherewith ye shall be able to quench all the fiery darts of the wicked. *17* And take the helmet of salvation, and the sword of the Spirit, which is the word of God.

Page 140- Ephesians 2:14

For He is our peace, who hath made both one, and hath broken down the middle wall of partition between us.

Page 142- Isaiah 41:10

Fear thou not; for I am with thee: be not dismayed; for I am thy God: I will strengthen thee; yea, I will help thee; yea, I will uphold thee with the right hand of my righteousness.

Page 144- Matthew 17:20

And Jesus said unto them, Because of your unbelief: for verily I say unto you, If ye have faith as a grain of mustard seed, ye shall say unto this mountain, Remove hence to yonder place; and it shall remove; and nothing shall be impossible unto you.

Page 144- 1 John 4:4

Ye are of God, little children, and have overcome them: because greater is he that is in you, than he that is in the world.

Page 152- Acts 2:1-47

¹ And when the day of Pentecost was fully come, they were all with one accord in one place. ² And suddenly there came a sound from heaven as of a rushing mighty wind, and it filled all the house where they were sitting. ³ And there appeared unto them cloven tongues like as of fire, and it sat upon each of them. ⁴ And they were all filled with the Holy Ghost, and began to speak with other tongues, as the Spirit gave them utterance. ⁵ And there were dwelling at Jerusalem Jews, devout men, out of every nation under heaven. ⁶ Now when this was noised abroad, the multitude came together, and were confounded, because that every man heard them speak in his own language ⁷ And they were all amazed and marvelled, saying one to another, Behold, are not all these which speak Galilaeans? ⁸ And how hear we every man in our own tongue, wherein we were born? ⁹ Parthians, and Medes, and Elamites, and the dwellers in Mesopotamia, and in Judaea, and Cappadocia, in Pontus, and Asia, ¹⁰ Phrygia, and Pamphylia, in Egypt, and in the parts of Libya about Cyrene, and strangers of Rome, Jews and proselytes, ¹¹ Cretes and Arabians, we do hear them speak in our tongues the wonderful works of God. ¹² And they were all amazed, and were in doubt, saying one to another, What meaneth this? ¹³ Others mocking said, These men are full of new wine. ¹⁴ But Peter, standing up with the eleven, lifted up his voice, and said unto them, Ye men of Judaea, and all ye that dwell at Jerusalem, be this known unto you, and hearken to my words: ¹⁵ For these are not drunken, as ye suppose, seeing it is but the third hour of the day. ¹⁶ But this is that which was spoken by the prophet Joel; ¹⁷ And it shall come to pass in the last days, saith God, I will pour out of my Spirit upon all flesh: and your sons and your daughters shall prophesy, and your young men shall see visions, and your old men shall dream dreams: ¹⁸ And on my servants and on my handmaidens I will pour out in those days of my Spirit; and they shall prophesy: ¹⁹ And I will shew wonders in heaven above, and signs in the earth beneath; blood, and fire, and vapour of smoke: [20] The sun shall be turned into darkness, and the moon into blood, before the great and notable day of the Lord come: [21] And it shall come to pass, that whosoever shall call on the name of the Lord shall be saved. [22] Ye men of Israel, hear these words; Jesus of Nazareth, a man approved of God among you by miracles and wonders and signs, which God did by him in the midst of you, as ye yourselves also know: [23] Him, being delivered by the determinate counsel and foreknowledge of God, ye have taken, and by wicked hands have crucified and slain: [24] Whom God hath raised up, having loosed the pains of death: because it was not possible that he should be holden of it. [25] For David speaketh concerning him, I foresaw the Lord always before my face, for he is on my right hand, that I should not be moved: [26] Therefore did my heart rejoice, and my tongue was glad; moreover also my flesh shall rest in hope: [27] Because thou wilt not leave my soul in hell, neither wilt thou suffer thine Holy One to see corruption. [28] Thou hast made known to me the ways of life; thou shalt make me full of joy with thy countenance. [29] Men and brethren, let me freely speak unto you of the patriarch David, that he is both dead and buried, and his sepulchre is with us unto this day. [30] Therefore being a prophet, and knowing that God had sworn with an oath to him, that of the fruit of his loins, according to the flesh, he would raise up Christ to sit on his throne; [31] He seeing this before spake of the resurrection of Christ, that his soul was not left in hell, neither his flesh did see corruption. [32] This Jesus hath God raised up, whereof we all are witnesses. [33] Therefore being by the right hand of God exalted, and having received of the Father the promise of the Holy Ghost, he hath shed forth this, which ye now see and hear. [34] For David is not ascended into the heavens: but he saith himself, The Lord said unto my Lord, Sit thou on my right hand, [35] Until I make thy foes thy footstool. [36] Therefore let all the house of Israel know assuredly, that

God hath made the same Jesus, whom ye have crucified, both Lord and Christ. ⁳⁷ Now when they heard this, they were pricked in their heart, and said unto Peter and to the rest of the apostles, Men and brethren, what shall we do? ³⁸ Then Peter said unto them, Repent, and be baptized every one of you in the name of Jesus Christ for the remission of sins, and ye shall receive the gift of the Holy Ghost. ³⁹ For the promise is unto you, and to your children, and to all that are afar off, even as many as the Lord our God shall call. ⁴⁰ And with many other words did he testify and exhort, saying, Save yourselves from this untoward generation. ⁴¹ Then they that gladly received his word were baptised: and the same day there were added unto them about three thousand souls. ⁴² And they continued steadfastly in the apostles 'doctrine and fellowship, and in breaking of bread, and in prayers. ⁴³ And fear came upon every soul: and many wonders and signs were done by the apostles. ⁴⁴ And all that believed were together, and had all things common; ⁴⁵ And sold their possessions and goods, and parted them to all men, as every man had need. ⁴⁶ And they, continuing daily with one accord in the temple, and breaking bread from house to house, did eat their meat with gladness and singleness of heart, ⁴⁷ Praising God, and having favour with all the people. And the Lord added to the church daily such as should be saved.

Page 152- John 3:1-7

¹ There was a man of the Pharisees, named Nicodemus, a ruler of the Jews: ² The same came to Jesus by night, and said unto him, Rabbi, we know that thou art a teacher come from God: for no man can do these miracles that thou doest, except God be with him. ³ Jesus answered and said unto him, Verily, verily, I say unto thee, Except a man be born again, he cannot see the kingdom of God. ⁴ Nicodemus saith unto him, How can a man be born when he is old? can he enter the second time into his mother's womb, and be born? ⁵ Jesus answered, Verily, verily, I say unto thee, Except a man be born of water and of the Spirit, he cannot enter into the kingdom of God. ⁶ That which is born of the flesh is flesh; and that which is born of the Spirit is spirit. ⁷ Marvel not that I said unto thee, Ye must be born again.

Page 152- Romans 8:9

But ye are not in the flesh, but in the Spirit, if so be that the Spirit of God dwell in you. Now if any man have not the Spirit of Christ, he is none of his.

Page 162- Joshua 1:9

Have not I commanded thee? Be strong and of a good courage; be not afraid, neither be thou dismayed: for the Lord thy God is with thee whithersoever thou goest.

Page 174- 2 Corinthians 10:5

Casting down imaginations, and every high thing that exalteth itself against the knowledge of God, and bringing into captivity every thought to the obedience of Christ;

Page 181- Philippians 3:13-14

¹³ Brethren, I count not myself to have apprehended: but this one thing I do, forgetting those things which are behind, and reaching forth unto those things which are before, ¹⁴ I press toward the mark for the prize of the high calling of God in Christ Jesus.

Page 181- Deuteronomy 28:6

Blessed shalt thou be when thou comest in, and blessed shalt thou be when thou goest out.

Notes

Notes

Notes

Notes